T0101036

HOW NOT TO Sell

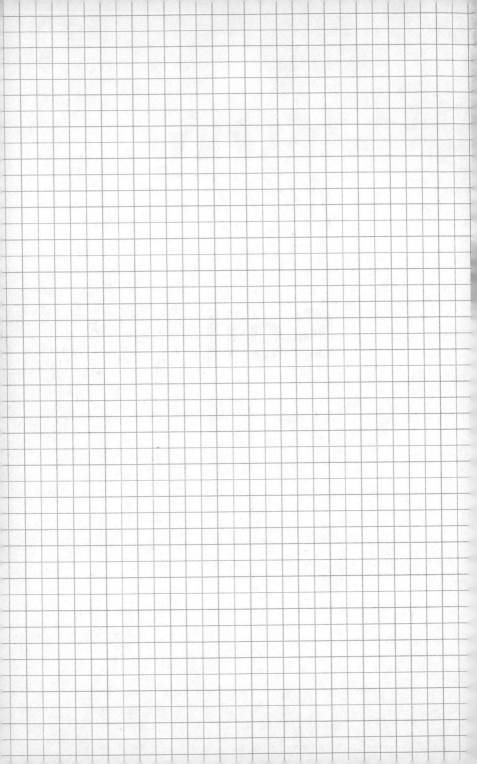

HOW
NOT
TO
Sell

*Why you can't close the deal
and how to fix it*

Mike Wicks

HarperCollins
Leadership

An Imprint of HarperCollins

© 2020 HarperCollins Leadership

All rights reserved. No portion of this book may be reproduced, stored in a retrieval system, or transmitted in any form or by any means—electronic, mechanical, photocopy, recording, scanning, or other—except for brief quotations in critical reviews or articles, without the prior written permission of the publisher.

Published by HarperCollins Leadership, an imprint of HarperCollins Focus LLC.

Published in association with Kevin Anderson & Associates: https://www.ka-writing.com/.

Book design by Aubrey Khan, Neuwirth & Associates.

ISBN 978-1-4002-2043-4 (eBook)
ISBN 978-1-4002-1890-5 (HC)

Library of Congress Control Number: 2020936143

Printed in the United States of America
20 21 22 23 LSC 10 9 8 7 6 5 4 3 2 1

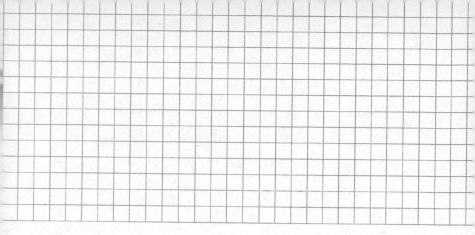

Contents

Section 2

It's All about What You Know

Section 3

It's All about the Sale

Introduction

Many years ago, I had a gig trying to help new business owners understand that selling was now a key activity for which they were responsible. Entrepreneurs who launch new ventures are often in love with what they sell; they have a passion for it, whether it's manufacturing wooden toys for children, offering a bookkeeping service, or setting up a graphic design studio. They incorrectly believe (at first) that their primary role is to manufacture what they sell or provide the service they offer.

In reality, however, they are in the sales business because nothing happens in a company until someone sells something. In small businesses, that's usually the entrepreneur, at least until the business grows to a size where it can afford a salesperson or a sales team.

Larger start-ups may have salespeople from day one, but even then the owner or owners would be wise to do some of the selling themselves at the outset. Knowing what prospects think of your product or service, and what objections to purchasing they raise, is invaluable.

Back to my teaching days. One of the first questions I would ask attendees was, "How many people here like to sell?" Out of a class of twelve or so, one person might eagerly raise his or her hand; perhaps another one, or two, would tentatively do the same. The rest would look as if I'd asked them to hold a tarantula.

The reason for this reticence toward selling always came down to the fact that they hated being sold to or had had some horrific experience at the hands of an oaf in a suit. The bottom line was that they disliked salespeople and that had translated to a fear of being disliked when they took on the role of salesperson for their business. I'd encourage the class to describe an awful sales interaction— in effect a "how-not-to-sell" experience. I delivered this same workshop dozens of times and the most common stories centered on people that sold things such as cars, life insurance, and, of course, anything where telesales were involved.

In most cases my students hated being railroaded by a prescriptive process; they felt like they were being placed on a conveyor belt that they couldn't get off of until they agreed to make the purchase. In essence, what they hated was fighting to keep control of the selling environment. Car dealerships in particular use this method. From the moment you walk into the showroom, you are shunted from person to person and given cost estimates to initial so that they can gauge your level of interest. Then your salesperson comes and goes while ostensibly "fighting" on your behalf with their manager. Then, of course, you have to sit down with the finance manager who attempts to upsell you with warranties and other options.

By this time, you feel battered and bruised and the best part of a day has been wasted. Most importantly, the salesperson is no longer your best friend. Now, this method does work to a point—they do sell cars, but at what cost? Talk to your friends; do any of them enjoy shopping for a new car? I doubt it. I, for one, have a five-year-old car and would love to buy a new one, but I'm putting it off because I dread going through the car dealership soft-shoe shuffle. I should say at this point that it's not only car salespeople that use this sort of prescriptive selling technique—it's common across many industries.

Just because a sales technique works some of the time, or even most of the time, doesn't mean it's good in your specific situation. There have been dozens of books over the years outlining techniques such as solution selling, strategic selling, consultative selling, relationship selling, persuasion selling, and even trust-based selling. Heck, at one time the Ford Motor Company used a method that encouraged its salespeople to focus on customers with large foreheads because it was thought they were more likely to be imaginative and open to new ideas. Good luck with that.

> ⌄ *There have been dozens of books over the years*
> ⌄ *outlining techniques such as solution selling, strategic*
> ⌄ *selling, consultative selling, relationship selling,*
> ⌄ *persuasion selling, and even trust-based selling. Heck,*
> ⌄ *at one time the Ford Motor Company used a method*
> ⌄ *that encouraged its salespeople to focus on customers*
> ⌄ *with large foreheads because it was thought they were*
> ⌄ *more likely to be imaginative and open to new ideas.*

If, however, you sweep aside all the rhetoric—all the systems, techniques, and strategies—selling is about the relationship between two people, and one of them, the salesperson, has the opportunity to screw things up at every step along the way. The world is full of salespeople who get it wrong more often than they get it right. In *How Not to Sell*, I'll share with you dozens of ways salespeople got it completely wrong and hopefully help you avoid making the same mistakes. What I won't be doing is promoting clever techniques or using buzzwords. In my opinion, selling is simple— it's the salesperson who makes it complicated or difficult.

HOW
NOT
TO
Sell

It's All about You

Sales are contingent upon the attitude of the salesman—
not the attitude of the prospect.   —W. Clement Stone[1]

Often, people in sales make life far more difficult for them-selves than they need to; selling is straightforward, people are not. In the next three chapters we'll take a look at the three golden rules of selling and witness how some real-life salespeople fell at the first hurdle.

Following the golden rules will help, but at the end of the day sell-ing is about how you handle the interaction between yourself and other people. In this section we'll take a look at why other people are so weird. That may be an overstatement, but life as a salesperson would be a whole lot easier if everyone were just like us, wouldn't it? In reality, it's important for us to be able to sell to those who act and behave very differently from what we recognize as "normal" or with whom we are comfortable. Understanding behavioral styles (ours and our customers') and learning how to style shift are vital skills discussed in Chapters Four and Five.

Section One goes onto to explore the numerous ways we fall into the trap of making it all about us, when it should be all about the customer. Chapters in this free-flowing first section cover topics as diverse as selling oneself first, punctuality, rejection, attitude, and commitment.

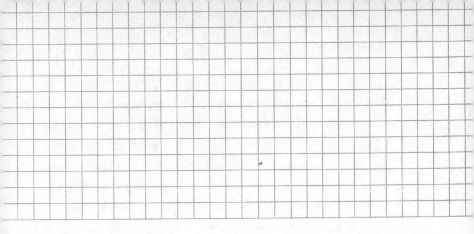

ONE

So, Who Cares if They Need or Want It?

The following story, and those in Chapters Two and Three, illustrate how easy it is to spend time selling to a buyer who will never be in a position to make a purchase. Selling to lost causes is time wasted, time where you could be selling to hot prospects.

> ∨ *Selling to lost causes is time wasted,*
> ∨ *time where you could be selling to hot prospects.*

BETH IS A thirty-three-year-old sales representative for a company manufacturing industrial cleaning materials, and she honestly believes she's doing a good job—a damn good job. She's chatty and popular and prides herself on her work ethic and productivity, but her sales manager is always on her case about her closing rate. Can't the jerk see she's doing her best? He should try being out there every day on the front line, persuading people to change suppliers and give her product a chance. Heck, she works more hours and makes more calls than any other sales rep on the team. She puts as much pressure on each prospect as she can, but in the end, you can't make people buy what they don't want, for heaven's sake!

OF COURSE, SHE'S correct: badgering people into buying rarely works and never over the long term. Beth's problem is that she is confusing productivity with proficiency; like many salespeople, put a warm body in front of her, and she'll launch straight into her pitch. She knows her product, she knows her competition; what she doesn't know is her buyer. If Beth spent more time targeting buyers who both **need and want** what she is selling, her closing rate would be the talk of the company—and that jerk of a sales manager would be off her back and focusing on some other poor soul.

If only Beth had realized that salespeople who plan more sell more, but more about that later. What Beth needed to do in the short term was to spend more time identifying prospects who actually needed what she was selling; if they also wanted it, or if she could excite them into wanting it, that's when she'd seal the deal.

A little online research—or a call to the company and a chat with the person on the front desk—is often all that's needed to discover whether the prospect is worth your valuable selling time. And yes, never undervalue the time you spend face-to-face with prospects and customers.

Like most things in life, if we spend a little more time considering our options, the more likely we are to be successful. What do carpenters say? Measure twice, cut once! If Beth was more selective with choosing whom she sold to, and if she deliberated over whether they had a defined need for what she was selling, the sales process would go a whole lot smoother and she'd be a top salesperson in no time.

How Not to Sell

- A warm body is a warm body; sell to them as if your life depends on it.
- Don't waste time seeking out qualified buyers; that reduces your actually selling time. More calls always means more sales.
- If people don't need or want what you are selling, you can always just badger the person into submission.

BUT LOOKING FOR people that have a need, and even a desire, for what you sell will only get you so far, as Justin discovers in Chapter Two.

TWO

So, Who Cares if They Have the Power to Purchase?

JUSTIN IS IN the middle of the pack when it comes to sales for his company, which sells automotive parts. He's in his mid-twenties and fairly new to selling but very keen and enthusiastic. When prospecting, he is careful to ensure that everyone he calls on has a need for his product, but too often he fails to close the deal. His prospects frequently refer him to someone else within the company, so he has to make additional visits, and even then, he gets stuck in a loop: they'll have to go "upstairs" to get approval or find someone else who can sign off on the purchase. This leaves him stuck in the "buyer's" office, looking at pictures of the guy's family and wondering why the heck he has a portrait of Mickey Mouse on his wall.

THERE'S BEEN A ton of stuff written about qualifying your buyer, and in Justin's case, his problem lies in his failure to discover whether the "buyer" he is selling to is actually a buyer—that is the person who can make a buying decision. There are a number of people who can look a lot like buyers but who may not actually function in that role.

Let's look at the cast of people who might make an appearance when you try to sell something; they may not all have a cameo role every time, but if they do, it's a good idea to know who they are and how to deal with them.

- **Initiators** are the people who may have called you or your office showing interest in what you are selling. Or, they could be the first person you talked to when you called to make an appointment. You should quickly establish a rapport with them; they might have a whole lot more knowledge, insight, and power than you imagine.
- **Influencers** might be tasked with finding out more information about your product or service, or they might be someone who has the authority to recommend you or what you sell to the buyer and/or decision-maker. Interestingly, an influencer can be anyone from a junior staff member to the buyer to the decision-maker's boss. Never underestimate the power of an influencer: treat them as you would an initiator.
- **Buyers** place the order. Beware, however, of buyers who are not decision-makers. This is the problem that Justin all too often faces; he thinks he is talking to the person making the buying decision, but in reality, someone higher up the food chain has to okay the buyer's orders.

When you're not dealing with decision-makers you don't have an opportunity to convince them of the benefits of what you are selling or the chance to get them excited about the purchase. It is important to know who is making the final decision—that's the person you need to sell to, or at least meet and bring onside. The key is to become familiar with the operational aspects of the company with which you are dealing.

- **Decision-makers** have the authority to place an order without getting additional approval. As mentioned above, they are often also the buyer but not in every case. For instance, if you are selling to the executive director of a not-for-profit, they may have to go to their board for final approval on the spend: although they are the buyer, the power in fact lies elsewhere. In this case, you would be wise to think of your "sale" as the act of getting the executive director to allow you to present directly to his or her board.

- **Users**, as the name implies, are the people who actually use the product or service. In Justin's case, he may not have to worry about users, but in certain circumstances a buyer and/or decision-maker may want to ensure that the end user is going to be happy with what they are purchasing. In these instances, Justin might do well to attempt to get feedback from users prior to making his sales pitch to the buyer/decision-maker.

- In many cases users are also **evaluators** but not always. Think of a manufacturing line where there are many people using a piece of equipment. The supervisor might collate feedback on the value and effectiveness of the equipment, or it might be a union or their representative. In fact, any entity collecting information would be an evaluator. The same is true in a retail environment where the users are customers and the evaluator is the store owner.

So, what can Justin do to qualify his buyer? The best thing is simply to ask his prospect, on his first visit, how the company makes its buying decisions. Isn't that easy? Unfortunately, Justin never thought to do that simple step in his early days as a sales representative. Before he went to see any buyer, Justin could have asked the front-desk person, "Does Mr. Smith do the buying for your company?" or, "What is Mr. Smith's role at Benning Brothers?" If you're thinking that the receptionist is too low in the office hierarchy to be of any help, think again. The person sitting at the front desk in just about any company knows where the bodies are buried; in fact, they often know a whole lot more than they should. If ever you need to get the dirt on a company, they are the person you want to befriend. You'll be surprised at what you can discover, and how helpful they can be, if you treat them well.

> ⌄ *If you're thinking that the receptionist is too low in*
> ⌄ *the office hierarchy to be of any help, think again.*
> ⌄ *The person sitting at the front desk in just about any*
> ⌄ *company knows where the bodies are buried; in fact,*
> ⌄ *they often know a whole lot more than they should. If*
> ⌄ *ever you need to get the dirt on a company, they are*
> ⌄ *the person you want to befriend*

None of this is much help to poor Justin, who is in too deep with the buyers he's already met. What he can do, however, is talk to his prospects about their team and the way the firm is structured. The more he can learn about the operation's organization, the more he'll understand who really makes the decisions. Asking simple leading questions, such as, "Is there anyone else you work with who needs to see this information?" or, "Do you need to bounce this off anyone else before making your decision?" can be the difference between making a sale and walking out empty-handed.

The answers to these questions will tell him a lot about who really wields the decision-making powers, and provide him with valuable background information should his contact ever leave the firm. If Justin was ambitious, he could take this one step further and ask whether he could have an opportunity to meet the prospect's boss or the CEO of the company.

How Not to Sell

- Qualifying buyers is a waste of valuable selling time.
- Who cares who the initiators, influencers, buyers, decision-makers, users, and evaluators are? Just sell to your contact. It'll all work out in the end.
- Ignore front desk people; they're know-nothing underlings.

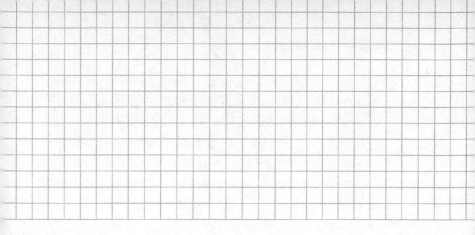

THREE

So, Who Cares if They Can Afford It?

I f Beth and Justin got together and compared notes, they'd probably learn from each other, but to knock it out of the park they'll need to add Sally to their group.

SALLY IS NEAR the top in sales for her company; she is careful to qualify that her prospect is the correct person to talk to and has the power to make a buying decision, and that he or she has a need for what she sells. But often she fails to get an order and gets frustrated that her prospect's company simply can't afford to make the purchase at this time. Her sales manager is not a jerk like Beth's; actually they're dating, so he can be a jerk sometimes, but not at work. (Please don't tell anyone! Their relationship is against company rules.) Sally sells high-end, high-output photocopiers but has a habit common to salespeople: her optimism can often overrule her common sense. A few months ago, she spent three hours with a delightful small business owner called Penny. Penny's company is doing well and is in a second-stage growth situation; in other words, it's strapped for cash. After Sally spent a whole morning pitching her on her company's equipment, Penny said, "Sally, I think you're great and the photocopier seems like an awesome machine, but we simply don't have the money right now to even finance it."

ALTHOUGH WE'LL DEAL with handling objections in greater detail later in this book, let's take a look at how Sally could have handled the situation a better. As we said earlier, she did qualify her buyer to a certain extent but then went down a rabbit hole, which wasted a bunch of time. A little research, a few questions, and a little understanding of her prospect's situation would have perhaps enabled her to arrange an initial, short, informational non-sales visit to Penny and delay her full presentation until Penny's company was more established. In that way, Sally could have played the long game, kept in touch with Penny, and been ahead of the competition when the company found itself in a stronger financial position.

If she was already meeting with Penny when she discovered the liquidity issue, she could have stopped selling, cut the appointment short, and rescheduled for several months down the line when Penny's company would hopefully be in a better position to make such a significant capital purchase.

If Beth, Justin, and Sally could learn from each other's strengths and only sell to people who want and need what they are selling, who have the authority to make the buying decision, and who can realistically afford to the make the purchase, then all of their closing rates would improve, and at least one of their sales managers wouldn't need to be such a jerk.

How Not to Sell

- Don't bother to check whether your prospect has the power to purchase. Sell to anyone, regardless of whether he or she has purchasing authority.
- If they "can't afford what you're selling," well, they're obviously lying. They'll find the money from somewhere.
- A buyer's ability to pay is irrelevant to whether you make the sale.
- Keep selling even if you know the buyer doesn't need, want, or can't afford what you're selling. Hey, you never know—if you're there long enough they might give in.

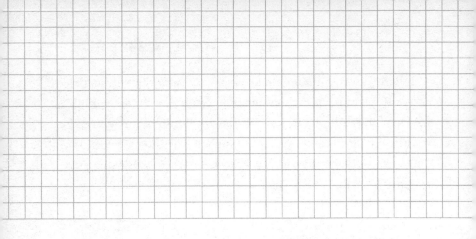

FOUR

Why Aren't Other People Just Like Me?

People have a cornucopia of personalities, styles, and behavioral patterns, not all of which you will naturally warm to. Selling would be so much easier if everyone behaved in the same way, wouldn't it? You've probably noticed that it's easy to sell to people you connect with, people you immediately relate to and who immediately relate to you—people just like you, in fact. But what about the rest?

Knowing your own primary behavioral style in your business life, and knowing how other people relate to your style, will help you get on the same page as your prospects and your customers. Whole books have been written on social styles; however, in this chapter we'll only touch on them briefly. We'll use them to demonstrate the importance of being a chameleon when in your sales role and how, with a little effort, you can learn to sell to any style, no matter your own. The power of being a chameleon should not be underestimated. Think about it: in your experience, is it easier—and do you normally sell higher quantities—to people you like and relate to, or to people with whom you have a difficult, even sometimes fractious, relationship?

⌄ *Knowing your own primary behavioral style in your*
⌄ *business life, and knowing how other people relate to*
⌄ *your style, will help you get on the same page as your*
⌄ *prospects and your customers*

BRENT, A SALES rep some years ago for a leading publishing house, was someone who really couldn't connect with anyone that wasn't a mirror image of himself. Most buyers disliked him; they only put up with him because he represented what was at the time one of the country's leading publishers. Buyers were forced to deal with him if they wanted to learn about his company's new titles and order its bestselling books. Brent was arrogant, analytical, and pompous and only related to people who were just like him—and there were very few of them. One buyer who particularly disliked him was an aristocratic English gentleman called Edward, who ran a small wholesale book business out of a very old building. He loved to tell the story about the time Brent was making a regular sales call and was in Edward's office pontificating on some topic or another while Edward was sitting thinking to himself, "Please, God, make this buffoon shut up." Suddenly the ceiling above Brent collapsed, showering him with a hundred years of old plaster.

Edward would gleefully tell anyone and everyone this story, emphasizing the point that the only part of the ceiling to collapse was immediately above Brent's head. It was divine intervention. However, Brent was furious and demanded that Edward pay to have his suit cleaned. Edward told everyone that it was the best money he ever spent.

BRENT WASN'T A bad person; he just became so invested in his own importance, and that of the company for which he worked, that he began to believe his own hype—a dangerous road for a salesperson to travel. Again, he wasn't disliked by everyone—there was one particular bookstore owner, who was also heavily invested in her own self-worth, who thought he was the quintessential publishing sales rep. The thing is, Brent could have been so much better, and sold so much more product, had he just been a tad more human and likable—perhaps a little more like the folk hero in our next tale.

TOM WAS A sales representative in the publishing industry back in book publishing's heyday; we're talking England in the late 1970s and early '80s. He was a phenomenal salesman, and all the bookstore buyers loved him even though at that time he worked for one of the smaller publishing houses. He was charming, intelligent, and funny, and he could relate to any type of person, no matter their age, gender, personality, or quirks. He loved people and they loved him—except one, perhaps. Stories about Tom's antics were legendary. On one occasion, his sales manager—who, like Brent in our previous story, was an arrogant, unlikable man—spent a few days accompanying Tom on his sales calls.

Tom and Roy were like chalk and cheese and Roy only put up with Tom's laissez-faire attitude and approach because his sales figures were always so good. On this particular day, they were in a small historic town with narrow streets; Tom was parallel parking his car when Roy started to open his door. Tom said, "Hold on, Roy, let me just reverse a little." Never one to take orders, Roy continued to exit the vehicle while Tom was focusing on his side-view mirror. When he finally came to a halt, the passenger door was wide open, and Roy was nowhere to be seen. Tom jumped out of the car and ran to the curbside, only to find Roy lying in the gutter under the car, thankfully unhurt. Roy never let Tom live that episode down, but Tom was a hero to the rest of his company's sales team, and the story earned him increased orders from the many buyers who knew and were less than impressed with Roy.

THE QUESTION IS, which sales rep would you prefer to be? Tom, whom everybody loved and respected and whose sales were excellent even though the company he worked for was only middle-of-the-road? Or Brent, who worked for a premier publisher but whose buyers barely tolerated him and who also—more to the point—only ordered the bare necessities from his catalog rather than taking a chance on outlier titles?

How Not to Sell

- Treat everyone the same. If they aren't like you, they're seriously weird.
- Be true to yourself and never adapt your personality or behavior for anyone.
- Only sell to people who are just like you (it's easier).
- Treat all prospects as if they are stupid or of dubious intellect—they will appreciate, or not recognize, the fact that they are being patronized.
- Reserve respect for those who see the world the same way you do.

FIVE

Why Are People So Weird?

om and Brent may be examples of extremes, but ask yourself, why is it that we get on well with some people the minute we meet them and have an awkward relationship with others, and then yet others still remain a complete mystery to us? What is it with them? Why do they act so strangely? Why are they so weird? The key to understanding this phenomenon is to first understand that everyone has a particular behavioral or social style. When you sell to people, you don't need to know their deep-seated personality: all you need to recognize is the behavioral style they are exhibiting in the moment you are interacting with them. Of course, you also have to know your own style. With these two pieces of information, you can stack the odds in favor of making a sale and building a good relationship. How do you do this? First, by tempering your personal approach to make them feel comfortable with you, and second, by delivering product information according to their style, in a way they can easily assimilate.

> ∨ *When you sell to people, you don't need to know their*
> ∨ *deep-seated personality: all you need to recognize is*
> ∨ *the behavioral style they are exhibiting in the moment*
> ∨ *you are interacting with them. . . . First, by tempering*
> ∨ *your personal approach to make them feel comfortable*
> ∨ *with you, and second, by delivering product information*
> ∨ *according to their style, in a way they can easily*
> ∨ *assimilate.*

Most people exhibit a fairly obvious primary personality, or behavioral style, but they also have a backup or secondary style, which is less important to recognize during your initial interaction. What are these styles and how do you recognize them? As mentioned, you too have a style. See if you can recognize it below.

The main personality types are: Analytical, Driver, Expressive, and Amiable. These were first identified in 1981 by David Merrill and Roger Reid in their book, *Personal Styles & Effective Performance*.[1] Since then, others have come up with myriad other terms, using animals, corporate roles, and many more, but Merrill and Reid's approach has stood the test of time and proved extremely effective.

Analytical

Analytical people make good accountants or scientists. They are formal and reserved and often dress in what some people might classify as a nerdy style, wearing checked, button-down shirts with a striped tie perhaps, or a tweed jacket with leather patches. Their clothes will be utilitarian, and they will not be fashion conscious. Analytical folks focus on the task at hand, the most important things being gathering information and the process used to achieve the end result. They proceed slowly and methodically and prepare carefully because it is important to them to be correct. They don't like surprises, unpredictability, or sudden change, and they hate to be placed in an embarrassing situation. When dealing with an Analytical you must ensure your facts are correct and present them logically. When uncomfortable, Analyticals become withdrawn and will avoid the cause of their stress. To get on well with an Analytical, you will need to encourage their thinking and show them that you are interested in supporting their personal credibility. In case you didn't notice, in the story earlier, Brent was an analytical and his backup style was Driver.

> ⌄ *Analytical folks focus on the task at hand, the most*
> ⌄ *important things being gathering information and the*
> ⌄ *process used to achieve the end result. They proceed*
> ⌄ *slowly and methodically and prepare carefully because*
> ⌄ *it is important to them to be correct. They don't like*
> ⌄ *surprises, unpredictability, or sudden change, and they*
> ⌄ *hate to be placed in an embarrassing situation.*

Driver

Chief executive officers and surgeons are often Drivers. They are businesslike and formal, both in the way they relate to people and often in the way they dress. They are fixated on the task at hand and focus on results. Their primary concern is the bottom line—the result—whether that is profit, saving someone's life, or winning the race. They are fast-paced and decisive. They have no patience for people who hesitate, are slow to make a decision, or who take too long to get something done. They like to be in control of situations, projects, people, and processes. Drivers hate losing control. They value themselves by their output and productivity, the results they achieve, and above all, by their track record. They are highly competitive.

If you put too much pressure on a Driver, they will kick back and tell *you* how things are going to be done. If you want to manage a Driver, you need to show that you understand and support their goals and objectives and show how you can help them achieve their desired result. You will need to be very clear as to how this will happen, by when, and at what cost.

> ∨ *If you want to manage a Driver, you need to show*
> ∨ *that you understand and support their goals and*
> ∨ *objectives and show how you can help them achieve*
> ∨ *their desired result.*

Expressive

Expressives make good salespeople, marketers, trainers, and facilitators. They are very open, communicative people with a flamboyant style. They can dress formally and informally, but whatever they're wearing will be stylish, and it will probably be a recognizable brand name.

Expressives love to be the center of attention—to be the first person to have the newest model of a flashy car, and they love having celebrities, even minor ones, as friends. They long for recognition and applause. They are usually well-liked and popular, although the other styles (except Drivers) often find them overwhelming when they first meet them in social situations. They are often excellent chameleons.

Expressives are fast-paced and decisive and like to be in charge too, although they are often quite happy to play backseat to a Driver. Drivers love to hire Expressives, as they share many of the same traits, but Drivers sometimes lack the relationship-building skills that Expressives use to great advantage, especially in sales roles. Expressives hate to be ignored and get bored and impatient with people who don't move along with things quickly, or who lack humor and enthusiasm. They become bored by routine and love to start things, but don't always manage to finish them. They equate success with the level of recognition and acknowledgment they receive.

> *Drivers love to hire Expressives, as they share many of the same traits, but they sometimes lack the relationship-building skills that Expressives use to great advantage, especially in sales roles.*

If you put too much pressure on an Expressive, they will fight back with sarcasm, sometimes aggressively. Their change of personality under pressure is the most marked of all styles (they can turn into pitbulls). To get them onside you need to support their dreams, gut feelings, and ideas and help build their standing with others.

Amiable

Amiables make good social workers, teachers, and nurses. They often wear soft, comfortable, flowing clothes in warm earth colors. Relationships are very important to them, and they will do anything to avoid confrontation. They take things slowly and easily and encourage an atmosphere that promotes close, safe relationships. They enjoy attention but do not outwardly seek it. For instance, at a party, they will hang out on the sofa until people come to them, at which point they will show their warmth and engage in discussions that are meaningful for everyone in the group. Amiables are the most loyal of all styles, as this is one of the ways they achieve acceptance; the other way is by conforming. They measure themselves by the depth of their relationships and the degree to which they are accepted by people. They pride themselves on their compatibility with others.

If you pressure an Amiable, they will retreat into their shell or submit, choosing to avoid the cause of the pressure rather than confronting it. Their change of personality under pressure is subtle and often difficult to spot. You may simply not see them again as they avoid your company. To get Amiables onside, you need to support their feelings and ideas and demonstrate how you can support their personal circumstances.

THE SALESPEOPLE IN the examples below are making things difficult for themselves and only effectively selling to a small portion of the prospects and customers with whom they interact.

Top salespeople know how to style-shift; they naturally, or have learned to, recognize the behavioral style being exhibited and shift their own to better relate to the person with whom they are talking. What does that mean? Here's a quick guide to the way you need to behave when dealing with each of the four styles. How easy—or difficult—that will be will depend on your personal style and your ability to be a chameleon. The most difficult matchups are opposite styles: Analytical and Expressive, and Driver and Amiable.

> ˅ *Top salespeople know how to style-shift; they*
> ˅ *naturally, or have learned to, recognize the behavioral*
> ˅ *style being exhibited and shift their own to better*
> ˅ *relate to the person with whom they are talking*

Review the descriptions of each style below and consider how you might change your body language, speech, dress, meeting and presentation styles, openness, friendliness, and other behavioral characteristics in a way that will relate better to each particular style.

If you are selling to an **Analytical**, you will need to:

- Be systematic, thorough, deliberate, and precise
- Focus on the task
- Be prepared to answer many "how" questions
- Provide analysis and facts
- Be less personal, more formal
- Recognize and acknowledge their need to be accurate and logical
- Not rush them
- Expect to repeat yourself
- Allow time for evaluation
- Use lots of evidence
- Compliment the precision and accuracy of their work

If you are selling to a **Driver**, you will need to:

- Focus on the task
- Talk about expected results
- Be businesslike and factual
- Provide concise, precise, and organized information
- Discuss and answer "what" questions
- Argue with facts, not feelings
- Not waste their time
- Avoid focusing on details
- Provide options using your expertise

If you are selling to an **Expressive**, you will need to:

- Focus on developing a relationship
- Try to show how your ideas will improve his or her image
- Be enthusiastic, open, and responsive
- Relate to their need to share information, stories, and experiences
- Be forthcoming and willing to talk
- Ask and answer "who" questions such as, "Who else uses this product?"
- Be warm and approachable at all times
- Work to minimize their direct involvement with details or personal conflicts

If you are selling to an **Amiable**, you will need to:

- Be relaxed and agreeable
- Maintain the status quo

- Be logical and systematic
- Create a plan with written guidelines
- Be prepared to answer "why" questions
- Be predictable
- Agree clearly and often
- Use the word "we" often
- Avoid pushing them into a decision
- Avoid rushing them
- Compliment them as a team player
- Be a good listener

How Not to Sell

- Bill treats everyone the same; you either like him or hate him and he doesn't care because if someone isn't just like him, then they're downright weird and they're not worth bothering with.
- Jane has an outgoing, confident personality. Some would call it over-the-top, but she is who she is and she firmly believes everyone loves her, or at least they should!
- Pauline chooses to sell mostly to people who are just like her: this way, she almost always gets the order. She is oblivious to the fact that she is only selling to approximately one-quarter of her potential market.
- Jake treats everyone as if they are less intelligent than him; talking down to people is his natural style. He tells things like they are and sees no problem with stating the brutal truth. He can't understand why this sometimes offends people. Like Pauline, his style works effectively with only a small percentage of his prospects and customers.

- Danny has a dominating personality and truly believes that the way he sees the world is the only way it can be seen, and he has little to no respect for anyone with a different opinion.

- Jonathon is quiet and unassuming. If a buyer has an objection, he always sees their perspective and agrees with them no matter if they are completely wrong. He'll bend over backward to give them whatever they need, even to the point of letting them walk all over him. He rarely gets good orders from Drivers and Expressives.

SIX

What Now? Sell Myself First?

This is a constant truth to selling: people buy from people they like. Consider con artists; they are untrustworthy, but they manage to sell people on an outrageous concept or "deal" almost entirely because they are likable, and of course convincing.

There are tons of things that can tick a potential buyer off—from tattoos and a Mohawk to a weak handshake, a salesperson who's standing too close and getting too familiar, or who doesn't make eye contact. In many ways, it's surprising that anyone ever makes a sale, given the minefield of social improprieties a salesperson has to avoid and the perceived slights they have to circumvent. But there are certain things that will undoubtedly always get you into trouble.

> ⌄   *In many ways, it's surprising that anyone ever makes*
> ⌄   *a sale, given the minefield of social improprieties a*
> ⌄   *salesperson has to avoid and the perceived slights*
> ⌄   *they have to circumvent.*

CARL REPRESENTED THE well-known celebrity host of a television series about antiques and was touting a book concept, based on the personality's popular TV show, around leading British book publishers. His cousin Phil worked for a top mainstream publisher and arranged for him to meet Reiner, the managing director, along with Sarah, the editor-in-chief. They were both pumped about the book and felt it would be a strong seller. Phil had pitched the book concept already; all Carl had to do was close the deal. At the meeting, Phil was embarrassed that Carl showed up a few minutes late wearing scruffy, overly casual attire. He looked as if he had slept in his car, whereas everyone else was in business formal. Sarah, while playing it cool, was keen to secure the book. Phil introduced everyone, and as soon as the pleasantries were finished, Carl, misreading the tenor of the room, aggressively made his pitch, overselling something that would have clearly sold on its own merits. Once Carl left, Phil hung back to hear what his colleagues thought of the book. The first person to speak was Reiner, who said, "I'm sorry, Phil, I know he's your cousin, but I don't trust him." He went on to explain that Carl's handshake had been weak, "like a cold, limp fish." He added that Carl had never once made eye contact with him, and concluded with, "And don't get me started on the way he was dressed. Did he come straight from a bar?" As much as the publishing company wanted what Carl was selling, they did not like or trust him as a salesperson.

In this case, we see a company turn down an obvious good deal purely because they felt uncomfortable.

THERE ARE A dozen ways you can mess up your first impression, not to mention the second and third if you continue digging. Every prospect is different so you can't expect to please everyone all the time. However, you increase your chances of making a positive first impression if you consider the type of person you are meeting and use your newfound skills to identify the individual's underlying social style and then style-shift to accommodate them. Think about it: you wouldn't fist pump an elderly buyer wearing a formal business suit, would you? If at this point, you're hesitating, you might need more than this book to help you increase your closing rate.

> ∨ *None of this is rocket science. Keep it simple: dress in*
> ∨ *business attire unless you are selling to surfers or*
> ∨ *skateboarders, and even then, be cautious. Give a firm*
> ∨ *handshake without crushing the person's fingers and*
> ∨ *look them in the eye. Be friendly and smile, be open and*
> ∨ *genuine. Don't fake it—BE all these things.*

None of this is rocket science. Keep it simple: dress in business attire unless you are selling to surfers or skateboarders, and even then, be cautious. Give a firm handshake without crushing the person's fingers and look them in the eye. Be friendly and smile, be open and genuine. Don't fake it—BE all these things. Too often salespeople launch into their pitch without getting to know the prospect first. It is important to allow prospects an opportunity to get acquainted with you and the company you represent. Show genuine interest in your prospect and remember: sell yourself first, your company second, and your product last.

Here's an example of one car salesman who got it wrong and another who got it right.

HARRY WAS LOOKING for a new car and was trying to decide which minivan to purchase. His children had gotten to an age where they were participating in several sports, and it seemed Harry and his wife, Linda, were constantly chauffeuring several kids with all their sports gear, from game to game. The time had come for one of them to give up their sedan for a people carrier and Harry drew the short straw.

His first stop was a Chevy dealership; as he pulled into the parking lot, he saw a shady-looking character smoking a cigarette at the entrance. When he opened the door to the showroom, the man dropped the butt on the ground, crushed it underfoot, and followed Harry into the showroom, where he introduced himself as Fred and handed Harry his business card. Harry half expected it to announce that Fred worked for Mafiosa Enterprises. Immediately, Fred escorted—or more accurately frog-marched—Harry to a highly polished, top-of-the-range Camaro. Oblivious to his protestations, Fred manhandled him into the car and asked a question only car salespeople of a certain age can get away with—"What have I got to do to get you into this car today?"—ignoring the fact that Harry was, by now, already in the vehicle. Harry groaned inwardly, and rather than try to fight off the oncoming tsunami of tired and clichéd sales techniques, he extracted himself from the car and hightailed from the dealership. As he drove off, he could see Fred was already back at his post, sucking on a cigarette by the front entrance.

It was several days before Harry could summon up the energy and fortitude to visit another car dealer—this time, a Ford dealership called Suburban Motors. He pulled up next to a bright, yellow, two-seater convertible Mustang with black leather seats. Head fully ensconced in the cockpit and entranced by the beautiful muscle car, Harry didn't even hear the salesman approach. He nearly jumped out of his skin when the man said, "Nice car, isn't it?" Harry looked around and said, "Yes, stunning," to which the man replied in a matter-of-fact manner, "But, I bet you're looking for a minivan." Harry was amazed and asked how could he possibly know? After introductions, Ron, the salesman, explained that given the clothes Harry was wearing, his age, and the car he was currently driving, odds were he was in the market for something a little more conservative than a roadster.

Ron spent the next few minutes inquiring about Harry's family, and they discovered that their children were of similar age, and in fact, the previous weekend, two of them had played against each other at soccer. Ron went on to explain the dealership was family owned and operated and introduced Harry to the head of the service department, telling him that whenever his car was in for a tune-up, they would wash and detail it free of charge.

Eventually Harry was the one to say, "Well, can we look at some vans?" In short order, Ron discovered that Harry couldn't afford a new Ford Windstar and steered him toward a used minivan that made Harry's heart sink. "I know, it's dog ugly, but it's got very low mileage, and it's under your budget," Ron said. Harry stood looking at the bottle green Aerostar in disbelief, gazing mournfully at the red go-faster stripes that announced it was the "Sport" version. Ron explained that its nickname was "The Brick" and that its "state-of-the-art" catalytic convertor was notorious for letting out noxious farts. But he assured Harry that it drove well, was in fact a very responsive, fun drive, and that it would house lots of kids and sports equipment. After a short test run, which Harry unexpectedly enjoyed, he protested, "But it's so ugly!" Ron smiled and gave him the keys and said, "I'll tell you what, it's Saturday afternoon, and no one is going to buy this today. I'll fill it with gas, and then why don't you take it for the rest of the weekend and see if it will do the job. Give it a good run up the coast, take your wife and the kids out for a day trip, have a picnic."

IN CASE YOU haven't already guessed, Harry's family enjoyed their day out and loved the freedom and space the Aerostar gave them—and Ron never got the keys back. Bright and early Monday morning, Ron made his sale. Four months later, he helped Harry's wife, Linda, replace *her* car, and two years later they bought a brand-new Windstar. In fact, they bought two more cars from Ron before he left the dealership and moved out of town.

Ron did everything correctly: he sold himself first, he sold his company second, and only started to pitch his product when his buyer was ready. He took notice of his prospect and assessed what he might be interested in and then qualified him in terms of his needs, wants, and budget. He was less interested in making a sale, and more interested in making a customer for life.

A prospect will make a number of decisions within thirty seconds of meeting you; those decisions will either make it more or less likely that they will buy what you are selling. Make a negative impression and you have a lot of ground to make up if you are going to get the sale. Make a positive impression, and you are already more than halfway there.

∨ *A prospect will make a number of decisions within*
∨ *thirty seconds of meeting you; those decisions will*
∨ *either make it more or less likely that they will buy*
∨ *what you are selling.*

How Not to Sell

- Buyers don't have to like you; they just have to need what you are selling, or you have to have the best price.
- My tattoos and Mohawk won't upset anyone—tats are now totally acceptable.
- It's old school to wear suits and stuff. Casual wear, even jeans, are totally acceptable these days.
- You have massive amounts of time for a prospect to get to know you; people don't make snap judgments about their salesperson.
- You are who you are! No need to tailor your approach to different people.

SEVEN

It's the Customer's Responsibility to Accept Me as I Am

So, you've bought into the concept of selling yourself first, but is that enough? The challenge is that prospects also need to be able to relate to you, and that might mean shape-shifting your personality, or your social style, to better relate to your prospect or buyer.

Think about the social style you exhibit when in a sales situation. What style do you naturally exhibit? And in a practical sense, how can you better relate to the person to whom you are selling? Think back to the earlier chapters where we discussed Analytical, Driver, Expressive, and Amiable styles. If you've jumped ahead and haven't read Chapter Five, go back and read it now, it's important. Even if you have, a recap might be useful at this point. In this chapter we'll take a look into the mind of a customer or prospect and then look at two examples of how to get it wrong or how to win the day.

Inside the Mind of a Customer

It's worth thinking for a moment about what goes on inside the mind of a prospect or a buyer. What they are thinking can either lead you closer to a sale, or further from a positive result. Here are a few of the things you might not want them thinking.

- Well, the rep from Blowhard is late—not a good start.
- Did he really just stub his cigarette out in my flowerbed?
- Is that guy seriously flirting with my front-desk person?
- Jeans? Man, either I'm overdressed, or they didn't make an effort to be businesslike.
- Wow, those are some tattoos and scary piercings! I'd better make sure we lock up well tonight.
- That handshake doesn't inspire confidence, and why did he avoid looking me straight in the eyes? Very suspicious.
- I feel like I'm in a *Seinfeld* episode—he's such a close talker.
- Is that body odor or cheap cologne?
- Oh no, now she's touching me—get your hands off!
- Does he realize that joke is racist, sexist, and offensive? Why is he still laughing?
- Ouch, did he really just use the F-bomb in front of my wife?
- He's launching into a political rant—shall I tell him he's insulting my political beliefs?

One of the keys to getting more people to buy what you sell is to get on their same wavelength; to be in harmony with them. Here are two stories; one is an example of failing to recognize the prospect's social style and watching the sale take a nasty turn, and the other is a classic case of the salesperson who successfully becomes a chameleon, style-shifts, and bridges the gap between himself and his customer. In both cases I am the salesperson.

> ˅   *One of the keys to getting more people to buy*
> ˅   *what you sell is to get on their same wavelength;*
> ˅   *to be in harmony with them.*

WHEN I WAS in my twenties, I was a sales representative for a paperback publishing house; for the most part, I got on well with the bookstore managers and owners I visited six or seven times a year when I was presenting my company's new titles. But one exception stands out to me.

I was visiting a children's bookstore owned by a large, slightly scruffy man who wore a long moth-eaten cardigan with leather patches on the elbows, all set off by tortoiseshell eyeglasses that were permanently lodged precariously on the end of his long Roman nose. He looked like a quintessential bookstore owner; he wouldn't have appeared out of place in a Harry Potter novel. He was fairly pleasant but immensely opinionated and didn't think highly of salespeople. On this particular day I presented him with an important new book on King Alfred, which was tied to a major new children's television series.

Normally this would have meant convincing him of the wisdom of purchasing a half-dozen copies—admittedly a big order for his tiny store but by no means impossible. It all went terribly awry when I didn't take into account his exceptionally pedantic approach to everything and his complete lack of humor, which clashed with my overly enthusiastic sales pitch. As soon as I started talking about our book, he brought up one of my competitors' new titles and noted that he hated it when publishers all got on the bandwagon and came out with similar books at the same time, just to capitalize on a television series. Having already purchased copies of my competitor's book, he told me that he wouldn't be taking my offering.

In other circumstances, I would have seen his point, but he was confusing the subject of the other publisher's book—King Arthur, the Saxon king—with King Alfred, the hero of our story and the subject of the television show. In sheer frustration I blurted out, "You've got it all wrong, they are two different kings. Our guy burnt the cakes!" At this outburst his face turned to thunder, and he shouted, "Don't you dare try to teach me history, you little whippersnapper." He then grabbed me by my collar and frog-marched me to the door and literally threw me out of his store. I landed in the gutter. Cars swerved around me, and a few moments later, my sample bags joined me. I'd misread this man's character completely; we were oil and water, and in retrospect and with maturity, I realized that I could probably have handled the situation differently.

By way of an epilogue, I should say that the store's name was The Owl and the Beaver Bookshop, and that the owner did send a letter to my sales manager apologizing for his poor behavior—which he concluded by telling him I was welcome to return and that I wouldn't find an angry little beaver waiting for me. What!?

I subsequently visited the store on one more occasion to show the owner I was not afraid of him, but after that, I decided such a small account with such an angry, rather large beaver wasn't worth my time or energy. I did, however, learn a great deal from him.

THE INCIDENT AT The Owl and the Beaver taught me a little about dealing with people who have very different personalities from my own. Still in my early twenties, I was very much the same Expressive that I was a few years prior, but I had learned how to temper the outward signs of my exuberance and shift my behavior to better relate to people of different styles. In other words, I began to know and understand myself and how people, especially buyers, perceived me.

MR. TAYLOR WAS an older gentleman who ran a religious bookstore called the Methodist Bookshop. By this time, I was working for a somewhat second-rate paperback publisher, and a significant percentage of what we sold was certainly not suitable for a religious store. Some of our titles included *My Bed Is Not for Sleeping*, *My Carnal Confessions*, and *Confessions of a Window Cleaner*. The previous sales rep in my territory had given up on this account, but I was young and keen to prove myself. I visited Mr. Taylor every sales cycle, and he was kind enough to look through my new offerings, buying an occasional western or something from our tiny nonfiction list. Financially, these visits were never really worth my while, but I liked Mr. Taylor and an order was still an order.

Over several visits, I noticed that he often had a magazine about music systems on his desk. I decided to buy a copy of the magazine and see what he was interested in, and I discovered a whole new world of high-fidelity equipment I never knew existed. During my next visit, I commented on the newly released Bang & Olufsen system, which was featured on the front cover of the magazine on his desk. I had read up on it and knew enough to hold a brief conversation about it.

This in turn led to a conversation about classical music, which I knew a little more about, and our relationship changed from being starchily professional to friendly. This went on for a few visits, until one day he asked me if he could see my stock book. Now, selling backlist items was always difficult even with my best customers—most buyers were only interested in new titles or current bestsellers, so I was quite taken aback.

He took my huge stock folder, which in those days literally consisted of thumbnail-size photographs of every book we published, and took a long while studying each page. He discovered that we distributed the *Peanuts* carton series by Charles M. Schulz. Unbeknownst to me, Mr. Taylor was a fan. This led to him installing a spinning rack containing a few hundred Snoopy titles in his store and also ordering forty or so other titles to try as standard stock items.

Mr. Taylor's account went from being more or less a waste of time to becoming an excellent and steady source of orders. The *Peanuts* series became bestsellers in his store, and, a twenty-something lad and a sixty-something man became business friends. I was even invited to bring my lunch and eat in his office prior to our sales appointments so we could discuss music and stereo systems. This is just one tale of many where building a relationship resulted not just in an increase of sales, but also in a customer interaction that was a highlight of each sales cycle.

HAVING SELF-AWARENESS AND understanding and accepting that people might see you in a very different light than you see yourself is an important factor to any successful sales career.

How Not to Sell

- Adapting your style to make it easier to connect and relate to people who are different from you just makes you fake. Be who you are and own it.
- It's up to the buyer to adapt to your style, not the other way around.
- It's too much effort to try to get to know prospects and buyers enough to style-shift so that they better understand you and what you sell.

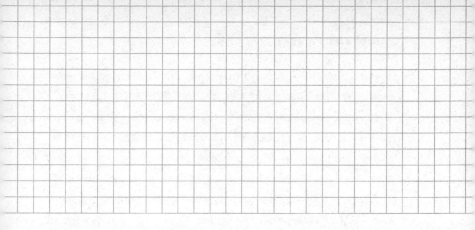

EIGHT

Hey, Being a Little Late Is Not Such a Big Deal

Being late for an appointment is a cardinal sin for salespeople and should obviously be avoided at all costs. It is, however, sometimes unavoidable or at least excusable. Wayne, a realtor, was horrified when he realized he had missed an appointment—so horrified that he almost got arrested when he tried to make it up to his client. We'll let him tell his story.

LAST FALL I booked an appointment with someone who had seen my sign at a listing. I was driving at the time so I couldn't immediately put it in my calendar. Ten days later, on the day of the appointment—in fact ten minutes after we were supposed to meet at the house she wanted to view—the new client called me wondering whether I was on my way. I thought, "OMG! The first time in thirty years as a realtor that I've forgotten an appointment!" The house was roughly a fifteen minute drive east from where I was, so I sped down the highway at precisely ninety-one miles per hour. How do I know how fast I was going? Because the nice police officer who pulled me over told me, even showed me on the radar gun. I was traveling twenty-nine miles per hour over the speed limit, so now I had to add another fifteen minutes to the already thirty minutes I was late. Oh, and $500 to my expenses. I arrived flustered and apologized profusely to my client and fessed up about what had happened. I couldn't believe it—she laughed, forgave me, said she actually felt sorry for me, and as luck would have it, she bought the house. Who says crime doesn't pay?

WE'VE ALL MISSED an appointment from time to time; we wouldn't be human if we hadn't, but reliability is vitally important to gaining the trust of customers. Wayne got it right when he did everything in his power to get to the important meeting as soon as he could after he realized his mistake. (Well, everything except for breaking the law.) If you are ever late, admit it, correct it as best you can, and never, ever blame anyone or anything else—even traffic—unless of course it involves a genuine emergency, such as a car accident.

> ∨ *We've all missed an appointment from time to time; we*
> ∨ *wouldn't be human if we hadn't, but reliability is vitally*
> ∨ *important to gaining the trust of customers.*

Now it's possible to sync all of your devices so that an appointment entered into your cell phone also registers on your desktop computer and any other electronic device you might own, and Wayne's mishap would have been entirely avoidable. These days, he could have simply used a virtual assistant to book his call while he was driving. Hey, Siri!

How Not to Sell

- First impressions are overrated: these people need you way more than you need them.
- Don't bother turning up on time—prospects are usually late anyway.
- Shun calendars and organizers; you'll remember that appointment.

NINE

I'm Top Dog and My Competitors Need to Know It

Arrogant salespeople exist in every industry; they usually, but not always, work for industry leaders, as was the case with Brent in our story earlier. As we observed, it's easy to start believing your own hype; humility is a valuable personality trait, one enjoyed by most truly successful salespeople. Here's a story about how much you can lose if you become as obnoxious as the salesman in our next story.

JACK OWNED A large neighborhood pub and experienced his fair share of arrogant customers—even one who barged past his wife and knocked her down a small flight of stairs that ran from the pool table down to the main bar area. That gentleman was nearly responsible for getting Jack into serious trouble; who knows what might have happened if three regulars hadn't been there to pull Jack off the guy? But every bar has its bad customers; that's just how it goes. What Jack wasn't expecting was total disrespect from one of his brewery reps.

Midmorning, before the pub opened, Jack would make time to see the wide variety of suppliers' reps that he dealt with. On one such occasion, he was sitting with Sharon, his wife and partner in the business, chatting with one of the reps, when a second supplier's rep turned up; he hung around at the front door, not wanting to interrupt. Spotting the second rep, Jack invited him to join them.

A little later, a beer rep turned up—it was Jack's main beer supplier. The vast majority of the pub's beer came from this one company. Rather than wait to be invited, this rep came straight over to the small group, sat down, put his feet up on the bench seat as if he owned the place, and started telling off-color jokes. One of the original reps excused himself, and the other followed shortly afterward. By this time—we'll call the rep Bob from Acme Beer Co.—was in full stride and dropping the F-bomb with increasing regularity. At this point, Sharon got up and walked off. Now that he was alone with Bob, Jack ran up one side of the guy and down the other; "How dare you barge in like that when I'm dealing with other reps, and while you're at it, get your damn feet off my furniture. And don't you ever drop the F-bomb in front of my wife; have some damn respect. Now get out of here and don't come back."

To cut a long story short, Jack complained about the rep to the brewery, who did very little to reprimand their salesperson. In the end, Jack discontinued every single Acme product—both draft and bottled beers, along with everything else that came from the company. This was a massive shock to the company, who thought they were unassailable due to their sheer size and importance in the industry.

THE LESSON HERE is that no one is untouchable; it doesn't matter how good your product is, how important it is, how well liked it is—people buy from people, not companies. Jack got some flak from a few of his regulars who were partial to certain Acme brews, but they soon found favorites amongst the replacement breweries' offerings. If that's not enough for you to see the importance of selling yourself first, then how about this? Jack owned the pub for another fifteen years, and Acme Beers Co. products were never allowed back. That one piece of rudeness cost the brewery hundreds of thousands of dollars. In sales, not selling yourself first can be expensive.

> ∨　*No one is untouchable; it doesn't matter how good*
> ∨　*your product is, how important it is, how well liked it*
> ∨　*is—people buy from people, not companies.*

How Not to Sell

- You don't need to build a rapport with your prospects; your product will speak for itself.
- You don't need to bond with prospects. Just get straight to your pitch and start convincing them to buy.
- Everybody's casual these days—no need for business attire; jeans will do.
- Prospects are like vicious dogs: never look them in the eyes.

- Firm handshakes are overrated; a casual soft handshake is just fine. Limp, cold fish hands and wrists are so in right now.
- Touchy-feely is in vogue; don't be afraid to get up close and personal. People don't mind you invading their space.
- Everyone likes a good joke, especially when you poke fun at minorities, politicians, religions, and other genders.
- Being politically correct is no fun! People will appreciate your offbeat take on the world. Go for it!
- A good conversation about politics, how attractive your prospect's coworker is, or religion helps keep it real. People want to know what you stand for and will respect you for your opinions.
- Make sure you put lesser competitors in their place, especially in front of customers, to let them know you are the top dog.
- My customers need me more than I need them. Our products are number one, our company is number one—we're untouchable, so they wouldn't dare throw us out.

TEN

Rejection Sucks—
Giving Up Is Easier

If at first you don't succeed, try, try again. Then quit.
There's no point in being a damn fool about it. —W. C. Fields

Around 90 percent of salespeople give up after the fourth call.[1] Statistics, however, show that when it comes to prospects, more than three-quarters say no four times before they make their purchase. This chapter explores the value of commitment, determination, and faith in the process. It will also discuss the psychology behind how consumers make purchasing decisions and why it varies depending on the product, service, and the age of the consumer. We'll also share a special mathematical approach to selling that can guarantee you'll always reach your sales targets. Unless of course you are truly terrible at selling—just being honest.

Rejection—or more correctly in this case, simply not getting the sale—demotivates most salespeople to some degree or another. Dealing with rejection on a daily basis and still keeping a positive attitude is one of the most difficult things about the job. Have you ever spent time cold calling? If you have, you'll have noticed a pattern: once you make a sale, the next few calls are not only easier, but often they result in more sales. Success makes us feel invincible. But get rejected several times in a row, and it feels almost impossible to make a sale. Rejection affects our attitude and we start feeling as if we're useless.

> ∨   *Have you ever spent time cold calling? If you have,*
> ∨   *you'll have noticed a pattern: once you make a sale, the*
> ∨   *next few calls are not only easier, but often they result*
> ∨   *in more sales. Success makes us feel invincible. But get*
> ∨   *rejected several times in a row, and it feels almost*
> ∨   *impossible to make a sale. Rejection affects our*
> ∨   *attitude and we start feeling as if we're useless.*

How do you cope with rejection—not on the surface, but deep down, psychologically? If losing an order or being personally rejected affects you, even a little, you will take that baggage into the next call. You won't be able to help yourself.

There are a number of ways to deal with how rejection makes you feel. If you have a strong personality, you may be able to separate past and future events. You brush the failures off and tell yourself what just happened has no bearing on your future sales.

That, of course, is easier said than done: the trick is to discover something that works for both your personality and the situation at hand.

One thing to remember is that consumers and business buyers buy at their own pace. It's easy to fall into the trap of expecting a quick sale. After all, from your perspective, the decision should be easy—but try putting yourself in your buyer's shoes. Consider how long it took you to decide which house or car to purchase, or at which resort in Mexico to spend your week vacation. Whether you get an order quickly or whether it takes twelve months will depend on what you are selling and the financial commitment involved. It may take seconds to impulse-buy a pack of gum, but choosing a new bed or sofa might take months, and in the process the consumer will have said no to several hopeful salespeople. It's important to remember that it's likely one of those "nos" might become a "yes" once all options have been considered. The larger the commitment, the more often you are likely to hear "no." The same is true when your prospect has a high degree of choice in their suppliers.

MARK USED TO sell books—not encyclopedias door-to-door, but forthcoming titles from a mainstream publisher—to bookstores. He was good at it and he enjoyed it; he had built excellent relationships with all the bookstores in his territory, but one day the company he worked for got bought out, and his boss called him with news that the geographic area he covered was going to change. Mark was furious that so much of the territory he had built over the years was going to be taken over by another salesperson. In a fit of pique, he resigned. He told himself that he was a great salesperson, that he could sell anything, and decided to change industries. He quickly got a job selling tools to factories and car dealerships. What Mark failed to realize was that he had spent many years in a sheltered sales environment, visiting the same customers several times a year and, for the most part, selling them something they wanted. To him, rejection was getting an order for ten copies of a new title instead of the fifteen that he had hoped for.

In Mark's first week selling tools, he heard flat-out "no" far more than he heard "maybe," and one heck of a lot more than he heard, "Yes, I'll take that." It didn't take long before Mark was spotted sitting in his car in a customer's parking lot after yet another rejection with his head in his shaking hands. On one occasion, while demonstrating a new repair putty that could set rock hard in minutes, he was so nervous, and his hands were so sweaty, that he actually dripped sweat onto the counter. The service manager at the car dealership shook his head and, without saying a word, walked over to the nearby washroom, brought back some paper towels, and wiped it up. Looking at Mark, he said, "You're in the wrong job, dude."

MARK'S FEAR OF rejection had exhausted all his positivity; his was a self-fulfilling prophecy. There are often more reasons for a prospect to say no than there are for them to say yes.

No matter how good your sales technique, you have to find a way to deal with rejection if you're to ever stand a chance of making it in the sales business.

TAKE BEN. HE worked for a company that sold subscriptions to a popular and highly useful handbook on environmental issues, policies, and regulations to contractors, consulting firms, and city planning departments. The company was owned by Ken and Deanna. Deanna managed the sales team. Once, during a meeting, Ken commented on how well Ben was doing; he had noticed that after almost every call Ben shot out of his seat, pumped his fist, and shouted, "Yes!" Deanna laughed and said, "Yes, he's good, but even he isn't making a sale every call." She went on to explain Ben's sales philosophy, specifically how he managed rejection. She told Ken that Ben had worked out that, on average, he made one sale every one hundred calls, and that that sale brought him one thousand dollars in commission. When Deanna had asked Ben to explain his fist pumping, he'd told her, "My colleagues celebrate every time they make a sale and earn a grand, but that doesn't work for me. I celebrate every call, regardless of whether or not it's a rejection because I know that call earned me ten dollars."

It's All in the Math

Here's Ben's simple math:

- 100 calls (including follow-up calls) results (on average) in 1 sale
- Commission on each sale = $1,000
- Commission earned per call = $10 ($1,000/100 = $10)

SELLING IS A numbers game; if Ben wants to earn more money, he needs to take more orders. There are a couple of ways he can achieve this goal.

1. **Simply make more calls.** If he currently makes four calls an hour during an eight-hour day over a three-day period, he will make ninety-six calls (for this example, we'll say he makes an additional four calls to make up the one hundred) making him $1,000 in commissions. If he were to increase his call rate by 50 percent and make six calls an hour (assuming his closing rate remains the same), sales would also increase by 50 percent and he would earn $1,500 without being any better at closing sales.

2. **Be a better closer.** We'll talk more about closing sales a little later, but for now, let's get back to Ben's simple math. If Ben found a way to increase his closing rate, say by demonstrating effectively how his prospects could save money by purchasing the handbook, he could increase his sale-to-call ratio. So, let's say that instead of making a sale every one hundred calls on average, he managed to make a sale every sixty-five calls; he would make $15.38 per call, or $1,538 every one hundred calls.

In example number one, of course, he has to suffer a little more rejection each day, but the extra $500 should help with that! In example number two, he just has to find a way to make what he is offering more attractive or be better at handling objections and closing sales, which we'll discuss later in the book.

The biggest misconception surrounding rejection is that the person you are selling to is rejecting you personally. That is simply not true, unless of course you are a truly awful person (just joking). For the most part, prospects are rejecting the product, the price, or maybe your company, and that can be for myriad reasons. Remember, making a sale on the first contact is rare; as we'll discuss later, perseverance is vital. You can take your pick from a wide range of experts on the average number of contacts you need to make before getting a sale, but one thing is certain: you'll almost always need to make contact with the same prospect on several occasions.

One of the keys to making more sales and reducing rejections is to become better at the *process* of selling. View every single sale, or non-sale, as a part of learning on the job. Use what you learn to fine-tune your sales technique.

> ⌄ *One of the keys to making more sales and reducing*
> ⌄ *rejections is to become better at the process of selling.*
> ⌄ *View every single sale, or non-sale, as a part of learning*
> ⌄ *on the job. Use what you learn to fine-tune your sales*
> ⌄ *technique.*

Sometimes, all it takes to be successful is to change the way you think, and so it is with rejection. No one gets every sale—rejection is a reality built into every sales job. The trick is to find a way to rob rejection of its power.

How Not to Sell

- Take rejection personally—very personally. It's you they are insulting.

- If you start the day with several "nos," just give up. That way you won't have to suffer being rejected again.

- If you don't make the sale on the first call or visit, don't bother trying again. It's their loss. And they'll never buy anyway. Most sales are the result of just one contact, so go for the low-hanging fruit.

- Don't look back on your failures, or question why you didn't get the order—there's nothing to learn there.

ELEVEN

My Attitude Is Just Fine, Damn It!

Attitude is contagious; if we are confronted with a positive, confident, happy, friendly salesperson, we are far more likely to hear what they have to say and ultimately buy what they are selling. Now, there can be a point where someone's positive attitude can turn into something obnoxious and annoying, but that's another story.

Think about it. Have you ever noticed that sales often come in batches? Do you remember the last time you got a good order and the very next call you got another? Is that just serendipity, luck, coincidence, skill, or is there something bigger at play? Could it be that you are simply sending out the right vibe? Could it be that your attitude is making the prospect feel positive about you, and that by some sort of transmogrification you are creating in them an intense desire to purchase whatever it is you are selling? Maybe.

Some salespeople report that on certain days they feel they can do no wrong—that they can, effectively, walk on water. Orders seem easy to get and are larger than normal, and customers are easier to deal with. Telemarketers know all too well that they can make dozens of calls without a sale, only to then get three in a row. Any form of cold-calling shows similar patterns.

Of course, the reverse is also true—we can't have yin without yang. If things are going poorly, don't they usually get a whole lot worse before they get better? Is this a coincidence, or does it all have to do with our attitude—our positivity or lack thereof?

From time to time we all blame bad customers, bad luck, the economy, timing, our product, or our service for our poor sales. In reality, the way we behave, the way we feel, and the energy we exude are far more relevant to whether or not we have a good or bad sales day.

It's surprising how often salespeople forget how their negative attitude directly affects their sales and ultimately their reputation. Let's drop in on Ruby, a salesclerk at a computer retailer.

RUBY WORKS FOR a high-street, bricks-and-mortar computer retailer and hates selling. Okay, *hates* is a strong word, but she severely dislikes having to stand on the shop floor all day and talk to idiots who don't know the difference between a Mac and a PC. At least, that's what she'll tell you at 5 p.m. on a bad day. On a good day, when she's sold fifteen computers and a bunch of peripherals and made some serious commission, she'll tell you she loves her job.

The odd thing is that she experiences more of the former on Mondays and Saturdays. Or is that so strange? Store manager Lauren has been watching Ruby for a while and has begun to notice Ruby's subpar Monday/Saturday pattern, although in truth, Ruby can act that way on any day of the week. Most days Ruby dresses well, wears an appropriate amount of makeup, smiles at every customer, and is just the right amount, and kind, of pushy—attentive but not intrusive. But on bad days, Lauren has observed that Ruby arrives with a sullen look on her face. She'll look disheveled and she'll have applied little to no makeup. On these days, Ruby exudes a negative attitude and is abrupt with customers, bordering on rude.

Lauren has overheard her say to a customer in frustration, "Do you know anything about computers? Anything?" On another occasion, Ruby exclaimed, "Why don't you come back when you know what the hell you want." Lauren has spotted her leaning against a shelf, sighing, and glowering at her colleagues, who were studiously avoiding her. Worse yet, on these days, Ruby has sudden bursts of frenetic energy where she follows a customer around the store, almost forcing them to buy something, as if trying to make up for lost time.

She's a Jekyll and Hyde character—one day a pleasant, competent salesperson and the next a liability. It wasn't until one of the other clerks mentioned to Lauren one Saturday morning that Ruby had really hit it hard the previous night that she realized that on Saturdays, Ruby was hungover. The pieces of the puzzle came together quickly after that, and with a little detective work, Lauren discovered that Ruby's performance was directly related to her attitude—whether she was feeling rough after a night out on the town, angry after an argument with her boyfriend, or ticked-off by an early morning run-in with a difficult customer. It didn't help that Ruby simply hated Mondays.

Lauren pulled Ruby into her office and they discussed how Ruby felt about working for the store before Lauren broached the attitude issue. Ruby was surprisingly open, and they had a positive discussion about how she might improve her attitude, helping her to not only make more commission but find more enjoyment in her work.

Some weeks later, Ruby attended the first of a six-week sales course called Hi-Touch Selling.[1] There she learned that attitude has everything to do with whether we have a good sales day or a bad one. The presenter, a short, high-energy English guy named Mike Wicks (author of How Not to Sell and How Not to Manage People), gave them—quite shockingly in her opinion—a task to do during their morning shower! At first, she thought "WTF, I'm not doing that; that's daft." But she really wanted to have more up days, and she definitely wouldn't mind earning more commission. If she could make every day a good sales day, she could turn her life around.

Mike suggested that every morning, while in the shower and waking up to the day, they take note of how positive or negative they felt. Was this a good day, or a bad day? Did they feel good about their life and their job, or would they prefer to crawl back to bed and pull the covers over their head? The attendees were to grade themselves on a one-to-ten basis; one being, "I hate life, the world is against me, I can't do anything right," and, "today is wonderful—nothing will stop me today," being a perfect ten. Mike went on to tell them that reality would likely fall somewhere in between, and that each morning, when they made mental note of where they were on the attitude spectrum, they should also remind themselves that it was within their control to accept that figure or challenge it. "If you accept that you are a five today, five will very likely be the limit of your success," Mike said, before adding, "But if you think about it for just a second or two and tell yourself it doesn't need to be that way—that you can be a seven, or even an eight, with a little encouragement from your inner psyche—then the act of thinking and saying it will affect the way you act and perform when you are selling."

Ruby remembers being doubtful, but Mike assured her that he had tested this on hundreds of salespeople, even some who had been working in sales for twenty or thirty years, and it really worked. He told the class that they shouldn't just believe him—they should prove it to themselves. For the next month, every day in their calendars, they should write down the first attitude number they came up with in the shower and also the number they felt they could achieve with a little effort. Then, at the end of each day, they were to also record their sales figures. Mike urged them not to fudge their figures—after all, they would only be lying to themselves. At the end of the month, they were to transfer the figures to a spreadsheet or chart and look at the relationship between their sales on days when their attitude was a seven or more and compare it those when it was a three or under.

By this time, Ruby had bought into Mike's idea enough to at least try it, and so she religiously recorded the three figures every day. One month later, she shared her Excel spreadsheet with Lauren, and after a few moments, both women were smiling: her sales figures were without question stronger on the days when she was a seven or higher. Even more surprising was that over the course of the month she had four outstanding high-sales days; and it was on those days when, while in the shower, she had given herself—or pumped herself up to—a nine or in one case a ten. She had literally cleaned up!

RUBY'S ATTITUDE PRIOR to attending the workshop had been contagious: she was like the wicked witch in a Disney movie who, with a flick of her wrist and a long pointy finger, hurls out a spell, only for the hero to hold up a mirror and send it right back, ruining her entire day. We are like that witch and our customers hold the mirror; what we project is what we get back. If we emanate bad vibes, they will return to us tenfold from customers and colleagues and even loved ones. On the days when Ruby was full of energy and enthusiasm, her customers responded positively and she made more sales—such a simple principle that can be so tough to apply when life gets in the way.

> ∨ *We are like that witch and our customers hold the*
> ∨ *mirror; what we project is what we get back. If we*
> ∨ *emanate bad vibes, they will return to us tenfold from*
> ∨ *customers and colleagues and even loved ones.*

How Not to Sell

- Your attitude is totally irrelevant to your sales performance. It's all about the product and the price.
- Most prospects don't appreciate positive, enthusiastic salespeople. Just keep it low key.
- Being a Jekyll and Hyde character keeps customers interested and more likely to make a purchase.

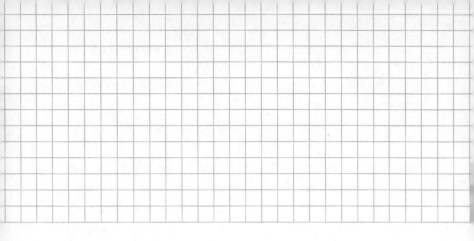

TWELVE

There's Nothing Wrong with a Good Whine

If we are up one day and down the next, we effectively take our customers on an emotional roller-coaster ride, leaving them confused and tired. People dislike unpleasant situations, and if your prospect doesn't know whether Dr. Jekyll or Mr. Hyde is going to turn up, they will choose to avoid the situation entirely.

Negativity is transferable. If you have a bad experience with a customer or client and you're not careful, you can carry it over to your next client interaction. This can be deadly, and it can happen without your conscious knowledge. Each sales interaction needs to be a unique event. Its outcome should not be tainted or preordained by past experiences. If you go into each sales situation with a high level of energy and enthusiasm and a positive attitude, you are far more likely to not only make a sale but begin to develop a long-term customer relationship.

The act of selling is a little like being onstage; as Shakespeare said, "All the world's a stage and all the men and women merely players." It's not that you have to be fake, or insincere, or lie, but you do have to play a part, no matter how you feel and no matter whether you like or dislike the person to whom you are selling. Imagine the prospect is an audience member who will only pay for the performance after the first act, or who could leave the theater at any moment if your performance isn't up to par. A good performance will warrant an order, while a poor performance will result in your prospect walking out (of the sale)—it's all in your hands. The bottom line is that actors can't afford bad days, and neither can you.

> ∨ *The act of selling is a little like being onstage; as*
> ∨ *Shakespeare said, "All the world's a stage and all the*
> ∨ *men and women merely players." It's not that you have*
> ∨ *to be fake, or insincere, or lie, but you do have to play a*
> ∨ *part, no matter how you feel and no matter whether*
> ∨ *you like or dislike the person to whom you are selling.*

Overall attitude is one thing, but some salespeople have a situational attitude problem. Stuart was in sales for half a century. Now retired, he shares a couple of stories about salespeople who somehow never learned the basic lessons embodied in this chapter.

I REMEMBER THIS one guy who was always ticked off by the news. He was a road warrior, one of those guys who back in the day drove from town to town visiting customers, staying in run-down hotels, getting drunk every night with other nomadic salespeople, and smoking three packs of cigarettes a day. He'd start off almost every call regaling his buyer with thoughts on why such-and-such politician should be shot, or about how the new DWI laws were insane, or how the Ruskies were about to take over. He had a negative opinion on just about every issue and wasn't shy about sharing it. In those days people put up with it: he was just seen as a colorful character. Today, that sort of interaction would see you turfed out of most sales situations.

Not too long ago, about three years before I retired, there was a woman on my sales team named Janet. She was bright, understood the product, and had good sales technique; she could certainly sell, but I always thought she could do better, so I arranged to accompany her on a three-day business trip. The first few calls went well, and I was beginning to wonder whether the trip might have been unnecessary. After lunch on the first day, however, we visited a longtime customer, and almost immediately she complained about the fact that she hadn't be able to find parking and that we'd had to walk "miles" to get there. If that had been a one-off, I wouldn't have thought any more of it, but I started to see a pattern. She whined to one customer about her husband being lazy, and to another about the rising cost of groceries, and to yet another about her sales materials—while I was standing right there in front of her. During the day, I had watched the buyers carefully, and it was noticeable how their open, smiling faces changed as Janet moaned about this and that, and worse, I could see their posture becoming tense. I could tell that Janet had outstayed her welcome, and although we always seemed to get a decent order, our clients were very obviously in a hurry to conclude the appointment.

A few months later, Janet and our company amicably parted ways. The new sales rep for her territory was an enthusiastic woman named Brittany; she was outgoing, fun, keen to learn, loved life, loved people, and guess what? Within six months she had increased sales on the territory by a staggering 48 percent, not only selling more to our existing customers, but bringing on a dozen or so new ones. Both Janet and Brittany were technically good salespeople; Janet undoubtedly knew the product and territory better, but attitude prevailed, and Brittany was by far the better sales representative.

BY SHARING THESE two examples, Stuart shows us that it's not always a pervasive poor attitude that can get us into trouble: sometimes daily life can interfere just as much with our stage presence. To the correct audience, hearing your thoughts on politics could be entertaining and a good way to start a healthy discussion. Janet's complaint about a lack of parking, for instance, would have brought about a level of camaraderie with other sales reps. But the last thing a buyer wants is to take on your problems. They just want positive news, period.

How Not to Sell

- Angry about something? Share it with your prospect. Everyone likes negativity—they're sure to be on your side.
- Wear your heart on your sleeve: everyone has a "whine" quota and sharing yours with your customers is a great way to get things off your chest.

THIRTEEN

Commitment Is Overrated

Commitment comes in many forms and the best salespeople are those who are committed to their company, their industry, their customers, the product or service they sell, their careers, and ultimately themselves. Unfortunately, many salespeople demonstrate little to no commitment to anything: this makes their job all the more difficult.

BRADEN WORKED FOR an established engineering company as a sales rep but was always looking for a new job. Whenever he met salespeople from his company's competitors on the road, he'd ask whether there were any job openings at their company and inquired as to what they paid. It wasn't that he was unhappy necessarily, but the grass always looked greener somewhere else. Because he was preoccupied with looking for other, better opportunities he never took the time to learn about the products he sold. When people asked about a technical specification, or whether his product could handle this or that job, he'd give them a brochure or refer them to the company's website. He was always pleasant, and his customers liked him, but they wished he knew more about his products, especially when it came to new equipment and technology.

On one occasion, a buyer told him that he was frustrated that Braden couldn't tell him if the new machine he was promoting could handle the workload the buyer's company required of it. When another prospect asked how long Braden's company had been in business, he just shrugged. That buyer decided to purchase from the competition. Braden never felt like any of this was a big issue. People bought from people they liked, right? One of his biggest failings was that he never really believed in what he was selling. He always thought his competitors' machines were probably just as good as his; it all came down to price in the end, or the deal. Eventually, Braden did find another job. He was very happy there, until he wasn't, and then he moved on again. The last anyone heard, he was selling timeshares in Puerto Vallarta, Mexico.

BRADEN LACKED COMMITMENT to his company, his job, his product, and his customers. He wasn't even really committed to himself either, or to his future. Salespeople like Braden fail on so many levels; they are like a house of cards. It may look good for a short period, but there's no structural integrity—everyone knows it's going to fail; the only question is when.

You Don't Owe Your Company Any Loyalty

Let's look at why commitment is so important in the sales process. First, if you are not committed to your company, if you don't have respect for the organization for which you work, how can you possibly come across as genuine to your prospects and your customers? Salespeople like Braden who have, and demonstrate, little loyalty to the company they represent will be quick to criticize it to their buyers. Make no mistake, this lack of loyalty will be obvious. The bond of trust between the salesperson and the customer will be broken, or it might never be forged in the first place. Once customers sense that you don't believe in your company, it makes them suspicious of the product and your commitment to them. They become concerned about whether you will be around to honor any agreements you have with them and offer ongoing product support.

Imagine that you've booked a romantic getaway with your loved one at a small country inn, owned by a charming-looking couple who have a beautiful golden retriever named Bear. The inn's website features dozens of wonderful images of the couple and a short essay about how they built the place themselves. The place looks perfect and you look forward to meeting these wonderful people—and, of course, Bear. Shortly after making your reservation, however, you discover that the inn is up for sale. How does that make you feel? Uneasy? Do you feel that they might not have the same level of commitment to their guests as the inn had in the past? Do their actions indicate that their commitment might be waning? You may start to question whether the inn is still operating at all, or perhaps you will discover that they've installed a manager to run the place and are getting out of the business. You might even consider canceling your reservation and finding somewhere else, all because doubts crept in about the owners' level of commitment. So it is with salespeople tenfold.

Without trust, long-term sales relationships are all but impossible. The result is poor or negligible sales. Reps who aren't committed to their company don't last long—not only within the company but within the industry itself.

> ∨ *Without trust, long-term sales relationships are all*
> ∨ *but impossible. . . . Reps who aren't committed to their*
> ∨ *company don't last long—not only within the company*
> ∨ *but within the industry itself.*

You Don't Need to Be Committed to Your Industry

Commitment comes in many shades of gray: someone might be committed to their company, their product, and their customers, but that's as deep as their dedication goes. The truly committed salesperson is involved at an industry level. They read the industry's trade journals; they follow what the industry's pundits are saying; they're knowledgeable about upcoming technology, new products, regulatory changes. Their commitment is absolute. What this means is that they not only have the answers to customer questions, but they can also passionately talk about the future of the industry and how it is going to benefit the customer down the road. This type of in-depth knowledge builds credibility, and credibility builds trust.

Take two salespeople: one who knows nothing about the industry in which they work, and another who is a fountain of knowledge and can provide valuable information and insights to their current and potential clients. Which one is going to be the better salesperson? Who is going to generate more sales? When it comes to selling, commitment is a powerful aphrodisiac.

There's No Need to Believe in What You Sell

Let's examine Sheila's story about buying a car—it illustrates the importance of being committed and believing in your product.

SHEILA WAS LOOKING for a new car: it was to be her very first time purchasing a brand-new one, and she wanted to make the wisest decision possible; she planned to keep the vehicle for a long time. Sheila viewed cars as a method of getting from point A to point B comfortably and safely—she did not see them as a status symbol, and she had no desire to go from 0 to 60 miles an hour in 3.5 seconds. She needed space for two children, and occasionally a husband when they weren't using the family minivan; she also wanted to "like" the car aesthetically.

She had shortlisted three vehicles: a Ford, a Nissan, and a Saturn (this was 1999) and she visited her local showrooms in that order. She took one look at the Ford and didn't like it, so she went to the Nissan dealership where she fell in love with a bright red Skyline. Mike, her husband, took a step back and pointed to Sheila as the salesman automatically started selling to him. Once his attentions were focused on the right client, the salesman opened the car door and ushered Sheila into the vehicle, doing all those thoroughly annoying things car salespeople do, like saying, "Isn't it pretty?" "Red is such a hot color; you'll really enjoy driving this vehicle," and asking what he could do to get her to drive away in the car today.

Extricating herself from the Skyline, Sheila turned to him and said, "Okay, tell me about the safety features," at which point the salesman froze, literally kicked the tires, looked over at Mike as if he could save him from this crazy woman, and then said he'd have to go and get a brochure. He then read Sheila the section relating to safety—as if women couldn't read. Sheila asked a couple of more questions before realizing that the guy didn't know the first thing about what he was selling.

At the Saturn dealership she was greeted by another salesman, who shook both her and Mike's hands and then asked who would be driving the car on a daily basis. Discovering that it was going to be Sheila's car, he gently led Mike to the coffee machine and suggested he sit and read the car magazines. He then questioned Sheila about what she was looking for from a car and the budget she was working with, all the time taking notes on a small, well-used notepad.

Once finished, he suggested they look at the Saturn S-series and took Sheila over to a midnight blue one and told her about the brand. He explained Saturn was a subsidiary of General Motors and that it marketed itself as a different kind of car company and operated almost at arm's length from GM. He went on to say enthusiastically that their philosophy was to maintain a relationship with the owner, and that this involved "homecomings," events where Saturn owners everywhere were invited to come together for a family picnic. Sheila was impressed that he was committed to his company, but what about the car? It was then that he made the sale, although he didn't know it at the time. Looking at his notes, he said, "The first thing you mentioned was safety; I'm glad because Saturns are some of the safest vehicles on the road today. Let me show you." With that he excused himself, coming back thirty seconds later carrying a car door with the interior exposed. He then demonstrated all the safety features hidden within in each door. Car sold.

Even though Sheila preferred the Nissan as a vehicle, she didn't feel comfortable with anything the salesman had told her—he'd known nothing about it, so what he said had no credibility. Was it a good car? Was it safe? Maybe, but she wasn't about to take the risk.

On the other hand, the Saturn salesman was totally credible; he obviously knew what he was talking about and the fact she was able to see under the "skin" of the car was amazing. The bottom line was that she felt comfortable and confident about buying the Saturn, a car she proudly owned for six years.

NEVER UNDERESTIMATE THE power of simply knowing your stuff and being proud of what you sell. Enthusiasm, passion, honesty, knowledge, and a good way to demonstrate it equal total credibility.

No Need to Be Committed to Your Customers

If you expect your customer to spend their money on what you're offering, you had better be ready to show them a level of commitment that overshadows that of any of your competitors. Here's an unfortunate story about a salesperson who let her sales manager convince her to go against her best judgement.

> ⌄ *If you expect your customer to spend their money on*
> ⌄ *what you're offering, you had better be ready to show*
> ⌄ *them a level of commitment that overshadows that of*
> ⌄ *any of your competitors.*

JESSICA RAN A liquor store with her husband, Jeff; it was a small enterprise with big dreams. They also owned the neighborhood pub next door, which was booming. One of their favorite reps was Kayla; Kayla lived locally and popped into the liquor store regularly to ensure Jessica and Jeff had everything they needed. They would sit and chat over a coffee, and Jessica would always support any new product Kayla was promoting as best she could. Unfortunately, Kayla's manager left and the new manager's focus was volume, volume, volume. He drilled into her that she should only spend time with stores that did volume, those that purchased large quantities of product and had rapid turnovers. As a result, Kayla stopped visiting Jessica and Jeff, even though she lived close to their liquor store and drove past it most days on her way to other sales calls. They felt snubbed and hurt—what sort of customer service was this?

MANY PEOPLE, ESPECIALLY people new to sales, find themselves in situations like Kayla's; they get pressure from management to sell more and focus on high-volume purchasers. The commitment shifts from relationships to sales units. But in order to be successful, salespeople have to walk a fine line between keeping their bosses happy and retaining customers. Kayla failed to do this, and this is what happened:

JESSICA WOULD SEE Kayla drive right past the store on occasion, and this started to bug her. After several weeks of being ignored, Jessica quietly stopped ordering anything from Kayla's company. That might have been the end of the story, but three months later, they opened another, far larger liquor store in another part of town, and later expanded their original store. They were now high-volume, but guess whose products were not represented?

WHAT COULD KAYLA have done better? All she needed to do was pop into the store once in a while to say hi, and ask whether everything was okay—perhaps tell Jessica she could call her anytime if she needed anything. Five minutes once a month probably would have shown enough commitment to save the account and all the potential business she ultimately missed out on getting.

Sales is all about putting people first: get the people part right and sales will follow. The value of establishing and sustaining relationships cannot be underestimated.

> ⌄ *Sales is all about putting people first: get the*
> ⌄ *people part right and sales will follow. The value of*
> ⌄ *establishing and sustaining relationships cannot be*
> ⌄ *underestimated.*

Sometimes it's all about rolling up your sleeves and getting your hands dirty:

ON THAT NOTE, here's a story from my own sales career. When I was nineteen, I got a job as a trainee sales rep for a publishing company selling paperback books in central London. Three estab-lished salesmen were responsible for my training, and it was their job to teach me everything they knew (and of course use me as their lackey). The oldest rep was John Abel, who liked to introduce himself in the following fashion, "Hi, I'm John Abel, Abel by name able by nature." I cringed every time he said it.

I did, however, learn a very useful lesson from him during my first week. John asked me to show up at a railway bookstall in Cen-tral London at 5 a.m. I was of course not a happy camper; every-one knew, except John apparently, that teenagers do not like to be up before the sun.

I did, however, arrive at 5 a.m. as requested (as if I had a choice) and was immediately instructed to remove my jacket and help un-load a truck full of newspapers for what I discovered was the bus-iest railway station in Britain. I was confused; after all, I was a sales rep, albeit a junior one, not a delivery boy. John and I both worked furiously for about thirty minutes until the truck was empty and the papers were piled high on the front counter awaiting the del-uge of commuters that would flood the station once the first trains pulled in from the suburbs. We then joined the manager for a well-earned coffee in the back office of the bookstall. Now, Lon-don bookstalls back in those days used to sell a huge number of paperback books—literally millions of people traveled through those railway stations every day. I enjoyed my coffee—laced as it was with scotch whisky—but I was still confused. After an hour of swapping very off-color jokes with the manager and some of his staff, the conviviality suddenly stopped; my trainer removed his sales folder from his large, square briefcase and started present-ing the new titles we had on offer that month. I was amazed by the size of the order. When we exited the back door, there was a line of our competitors' salespeople waiting their turn. The old rep looked at me and said, "Guess who got first dibs on Fred's monthly book-buying budget?" It was then that I realized the reason for the early start and the little bit of laboring.

MR. ABEL WAS committed to his customers—sure, he had an ulterior motive, but that's not how the habit of helping to unload the truck started. A few months prior to the events described above, the manager had mentioned that he had a bad back, but he always felt he should help his "lads" unload in the mornings. Without saying anything, once or twice a month, John would just turn up, help unload the truck, and leave. The manager never forgot John's commitment and John never got a poor order—in fact, our imprint's exposure at the bookstall far outweighed its true status in the hierarchy of publishing firms represented.

No Need to Be Committed to Your Sales Career

Almost anyone can sell to some degree, but those who excel at it are often those who love selling. They live for the chase, they like dealing with people, like helping people—for these reps it's never a chore, or just a job, it's part of who they are.

NICOLE, TWENTY-EIGHT years old, worked as a sales rep for a large, well-established stationery company; her job was to present and sell new card designs and other products to existing customers while at the same time show the product line to new customers, tell them about the company's current promotions, and share company news. She would sit with buyers and take them through her portfolio and samples; in this way buyers could intimately connect with the product—actually see it and feel the quality of the paper. Nicole symbolically took her company to the retailer. She was good at her job and would enthusiastically show buyers the company's bestselling stationary and make suggestions based on the type of store it was and its customer demographic. And, of course, she took orders.

She was likable, popular, and keen to demonstrate and advise buyers how they could increase sales. This consultancy role in selling is powerful—Nicole was truly invested in her customers' successes. She did a great job in keeping both her customers up to date with current manufacturing and industry trends, while also reporting back to the head office on what buyers were saying about her company's product line and the market in general. She would also pay close attention to her competition and report back to her boss regularly on what she saw.

As a team member, she felt she played her part, but at her last employee evaluation, her manager, Megan, said she felt Nicole could do more, that her sales were not keeping pace with many of her colleagues. Her call rate was the lowest in the sales team. Nicole countered with, "I am supposed to do at least eight calls a day and that's what I always do!" Megan referred to a report she had placed beside her on the desk and said, "Yes, but on average, your colleagues are doing ten calls a day." Nicole's reply was reflective of the attitude of those who ensure proper work-life balance: "But I have a life."

The reality was that Nicole was a highly efficient and effective sales rep. She would plan her calls weeks in advance, grouping

> them geographically to minimize the time it took to get there. In this way she could do the proscribed eight calls a day and still enjoy a glass of wine on her deck at home, or in the bar at her hotel on longer trips, by 5 p.m. every evening. Work-life balance was all-important to Nicole and she fiercely protected her "playtime."

ON THE FACE of it, there is nothing wrong with the way Nicole was handling her sales job; she was doing the bare minimum required to satisfy her company and what she did do, she did well. But does this make her a top-notch salesperson? Will it further her career or hinder it? Her answer would probably be that she does enough, she does what the company expects of her, and she'd be correct. The problem lies in the fact that her colleagues were more productive; they earned more and were more likely to be promoted when an opportunity arose. We said earlier that sales and selling are about people, not units and dollars, but in truth it's about both. By focusing on people, the units and dollars will follow because the more people we have a relationship with, the more sales we will make.

If the title of this book, *How Not to Sell*, were phrased as a question, one answer would be, "Don't make calls," or "Make fewer calls." Nicole is an excellent salesperson in terms of personality and sales technique, but if she did two more calls a day her productivity would rise by a healthy 25 percent and her sales figures would rise accordingly. Not only that, her manager would be very happy, and with all the extra commission, Nicole might soon be sitting by the pool at a five-star Mexican resort with her glass of wine instead of sitting on her deck.

Nicole was good at what she did, but she wasn't really committed to her job. More importantly, she wasn't committed to selling;

perhaps she didn't enjoy it enough. Maybe, and this happens, it simply wasn't sufficiently demanding. One way to be successful in your sales career is to find ways to challenge yourself.

Salespeople who have a true commitment to selling have a different mindset. To them, selling is like a competition—they need to be the number one rep on the team or at the company. They need to see their products front and center in their customers' displays. In Chapter Fifteen, we'll talk about targeting and how targeting yourself can help you become top dog.

> ∨ *Salespeople who have a true commitment to selling*
> ∨ *have a different mindset. To them, selling is like a*
> ∨ *competition—they need to be the number one rep on*
> ∨ *the team or at the company.*

How Not to Sell

- Customers don't care whether you are loyal to your company, and who cares if they do? It's not as if they're going to trust you any more just because you believe in your company and its products.
- Fake being genuine. Buyers will never know the difference.
- Let other reps waste their time becoming involved in the industry—it won't give them any advantage.
- Enthusiasm, passion, honesty, and knowledge don't help with credibility. You have the best product and buyers know it.
- Don't waste time learning about your products. You can always refer customers to the brochure or the company website.

- Ignore smaller customers—only look after your high-volume clients.
- Loyalty to your company is a mug's game; you should always be looking for better opportunities with your company's competition.
- You don't have to love selling, or even plan to stay in sales, to be good at it—anyone can sell and be good at it, it's easy.
- Selling is just a way to make money; it's not a lifetime job or anything. Make your job fit around your life, not the other way around.
- Do just enough to keep your sales manager off your back. Keeping your head down is a powerful tool and career enhancer.

FOURTEEN

Doing Extra Calls Is a Mug's Game

Nicole, in our story above, couldn't wait until she was done for the day. She worked more efficiently just so she could sign-off early. Here's a story about her opposite, a sales rep who couldn't stop thinking about the next sale:

ANANYA SOLD JEWELRY—mostly gold, mostly high-end, along with a fashionable mid-range selection of men's and womens' watches. When she joined the wholesale jewelry company, she took over an existing territory that consisted of 122 jewelry stores. The previous rep hadn't looked after the area very well, but at least they had regularly visited each store every six to eight weeks.

Selling expensive jewelry wasn't something that could be rushed, so most reps in the company managed four calls a day. A little over seven weeks after taking over the territory, Ananya had managed to visit almost all of her accounts, but still had to revisit about a dozen who for one reason or another had not been there when she called, or whom she'd been unable to reach when she had contacted them to book an appointment.

On days when she was revisiting clients, she found that, for the most part, she had only three appointments so by midafternoon she was usually heading home. During her third month with the company, she experienced such a day and was driving home when she spotted a wholesale warehouse on the outskirts of a major city. On a whim she decided to pop in and check it out. In the parking lot there were more than a smattering of high-end cars: Mercedes, BMWs, Lexuses, Porsches, and even the occasional Bentley. She walked in and was immediately asked for her membership card (it was similar to a Costco store); she told the person she wasn't a member but would like to speak to the manager and was asked to wait. For the next few minutes she stood and watched as people left with thousands of dollars' worth of products, destined, she imagined, for corner stores and small grocers. As luck would have it, the manager wasn't busy and agreed to see her. She told him who she was, who she worked for, and what she sold. She pitched her range of watches, telling him that they could be perfect for his clientele and that she would be able to supply him, at no cost, with a display counter. She had even found the perfect spot for it: a small space in a great location that was currently unused and therefore not earning any revenue for his company. Walking out the door an hour later, she couldn't believe she had just sold, albeit initially on consignment for a trial run, $30,000 worth of watches.

That was a turning point for Ananya: from that day forward, anytime she was leaving a town or city with enough time to spare she'd commit to making a cold call. In truth, most of the time she got rebuffed, but on average she managed to get one, sometimes two, new clients a month. Those new clients increased her territory's revenues by an amazing 17.5 percent. By way of an epilogue, the watches she sold to the original warehouse took off so well that the store is now one of her best customers. Of course, being a trailblazer does have its drawbacks: other watch suppliers caught onto her idea and now she has to share space with several other companies.

ANANYA'S STORY IS a wonderful example of the "one more call" principle. Most, if not all, businesses suffer from attrition—the loss of customers for one reason or another. Stores close down, move locations, change hands, rework product ranges, or are sold to a competitor; often there is nothing you can do except grin and bear it gracefully. Someone once said, if a business is not moving forward, it's moving backward: there is never a chance of maintaining the status quo. If you are in sales, you need to constantly be looking to grow your customer base or you will eventually find yourself out of a job.

∨ *Stores close down, move locations, change hands,*
∨ *rework product ranges, or are sold to a competitor;*
∨ *often there is nothing you can do except grin and bear*
∨ *it gracefully. . . . If you are in sales, you need to*
∨ *constantly be looking to grow your customer base or*
∨ *you will eventually find yourself out of a job.*

How Not to Sell

- The "one more call" philosophy is a myth. You'd probably screw it up or get rejected anyway.
- Only do what's required of you—nobody respects a suck-up.
- If you finish your last sales call of the day early, take some time off and relax. There's a cold beer in the fridge at home with your name on it and you deserve it; save your energy for tomorrow.

FIFTEEN

I Hate Targets.
They Are So Bogus

Sales targets are a bone of contention with many salespeople. The idea behind them is to motivate members of a team to sell more, and they will usually earn a bonus or commission by doing so. Unfortunately, many sales targets are set unrealistically high and ultimately demotivate people, causing animosity within the team and with management. There is a wonderful story about sales targets attributed to Jim Pattison, a rags-to-riches Canadian business magnate and philanthropist, who is listed by *Canadian Business* magazine as one of the top twenty wealthiest people in Canada. Today, he is in his early nineties, but when he was in his mid-twenties, he managed a car lot and initiated a policy whereby the poorest performing salesman (and in those days they were all men) was fired at the end of every month. Motivation comes in many forms, and certainly every member of Pattison's sales team was eager not to end up in last place at the end of the month.

Bottom line? The highest performing salespeople are those who love sales targets. They find it exciting and rewarding to strive toward something and even go beyond the goal to become top salesperson. The people who were at the bottom of the pack in Jim's sales team were probably coasting along rather than challenging themselves and were quite possibly also in the wrong career.

> ∨   *The highest performing salespeople are those who*
> ∨   *love sales targets. They find it exciting and rewarding*
> ∨   *to strive toward something and even go beyond the*
> ∨   *goal to become top salesperson.*

Super salespeople are those who set their own targets over and above what their sales manager has set. How you target yourself, and what you target, will depend on whether you are an inside or outside sales rep and whether your business is B2B (business-to-business) or B2C (business-to-consumer). Other sales roles such as business development, sometimes called prospecting reps, will also require their own specific set of targets.

Here are some ways in which you can set targets to challenge yourself. Remember, reps who self-target, sell more—exponentially more.

- **Target how many calls you do per hour, day, week, and month.** These numbers could be dozens if you are in telesales and we're talking contacts, to maybe six to ten if you are out in the field. The key is to know how you are currently performing and add a percentage, or perhaps take the average number of calls your team makes and come up with a number that's even higher. Remember what we said earlier about sales being, at least in part, a numbers game? An increase in calls will almost always result in an increase in sales even if you don't manage to improve your closing rate. Targeting this way will also encourage you to work smarter so you're not just working longer hours. To achieve this you may need to think about how you sell and look toward how you can improve your sales technique.

- In the same way that you can challenge yourself with unit targets, you can also **use the dollar value as a metric.** In both cases, you can set targets based on increasing your own sales numbers, or you can use the averages across the rest of your sales team or even across your entire company.

- If most of your calls are to existing customers, as is often the case with a B2B outside sales rep, **task yourself with making a set number of cold calls per week.** Making more cold calls is one of the top ways you can not only increase your current sales but also build the future of your territory or business.

- If you have decided to increase the number of calls you make over a period of time, also **try targeting how many new accounts, or new customers, you sign-up.** The two go hand-in-hand and feed off each other.

- **Targeting your closing rate can offer you an opportunity for long-term sales and career growth.** If you are currently closing one prospect out of ten and you increase that to two, you are doubling your success rate. Imagine the effect that will have on your sales figures. Once you are comfortable with your new closing rate, increase it again—this is a target strategy that keeps on giving.

- **There are more ways to increase revenue than just being more productive or improving your technique.** Try targeting your attrition rate, sometimes called churn rate. If customer loyalty is a challenge in your industry, or within your company, you can make a significant long-term impact on territory revenues by keeping your customers happy. Discover your territory's attrition rate and focus on reducing it—every customer you keep is one you won't have to replace. Retaining the revenue of existing customers, those you have worked hard in the past to service, makes sense especially when you consider their potential revenue value over, say, the next five years.

- **In some industries companies are obliged to accept returns, or unsold goods.** This can have a significant impact on the profitability of a salesperson's territory and ultimately their earning potential. Targeting a reduction in your "returns" percentage by selling smarter (i.e., not overselling) can have a significant impact on total sales revenue.

- **The key to using targeting to incentivize yourself is to use your imagination to find a way to make it exciting.** Some salespeople have been known to target the number of window or in-store product displays they can obtain. In one case, a salesman in the British publishing industry managed to get twenty bookstores to feature his company's lead title of the month in window displays across his territory. This feat resulted in he and his company being featured in *The Bookseller*, a leading trade magazine, which in turn resulted in increased interest in the book and even more sales. As an added bonus, the sales representative in question received several offers of employment from other leading publishers.

∨ *The key to using targeting to incentivize yourself is to*
∨ *use your imagination to find a way to make it exciting.*

How Not to Sell

- If I do more calls, that doesn't mean I'll make sales—it just means I have to work harder.
- I already do too many calls; the last thing I want to do is work more hours.
- Cold calls are where salespeople go to die; they're not in my job description.
- My sales technique is just fine. Taking additional training or looking for ways to close more sales is just a waste of time.
- Losing an occasional customer here and there is one of the costs of doing business. There's no need to be concerned.
- Don't push yourself by setting yourself targets—that's for suck-ups and geeks.
- It's my boss's job to set targets, not mine.
- If you're a sales manager, set sales targets unrealistically high to motivate your salespeople, and fire the weakest performer every month.

It's All about What You Know

Knowledge is power? No. Knowledge on its own is nothing, but the application of useful knowledge, now that is powerful. —Rob Liano[1]

The quote above sums up what we will cover in the following nine chapters. In Section One we looked at the personal behavior, attitude, and commitment of you the salesperson. In Section Two we'll focus on what you need to know about your customer, product, industry, market, and your competition to give you an edge over all the other companies fighting for a share of the market in your territory—be that an entire region, state, or your individual retail store. Truly great salespeople are often those who are curious, the ones who are always wondering "what if?" and looking for new opportunities.

They are also information junkies, eager to learn and improve—the people who are willing to read a magazine that focuses on something they have no interest in, just to get a different perspective, and then adapt it to bring about change in their job, company, or industry.

In this section, we'll also deal with the power of planning a sales call, clearly understanding your objectives, and the importance of keeping records.

To a certain extent, we live in a very surface-oriented society. Find a prospect, pitch them, make a sale or not, then move on. That takes a lot of work and echoes the disposable world we live in today. But what would the world look like if we sold in a way that builds long-term mutually beneficial relationships?

SIXTEEN

Are You Kidding? Knowledge Isn't Power

In Chapter Ten we talked about Mark, the rep who in a fit of pique decided to quit his job in an industry he knew well only to start afresh in one he knew nothing about. If you remember, in his new job, Mark lacked any real knowledge of his products or how they were used. This lack of knowledge spread beyond his product to his industry; he was out of his depth, and that left him a nervous wreck with sweating hands dripping on a buyer's countertop. We also saw Sheila, in Chapter Fourteen, decide not to purchase a car she liked because the salesman's lack of knowledge failed to instill confidence in the product. Instead she bought from someone who had all the answers.

There are two things at play here; first was the fear and trepidation the salesman felt from his lack of knowledge, and second was the credibility gap between a knowledgeable salesperson and one who was simply going through the motions. As Ralph Waldo Emerson said, "Knowledge is the antidote to fear."

An exercise, used by trainers who teach public speaking workshops, encourages people petrified of public speaking to talk about something they are passionate about. Topics can include grandchildren, pets, or their hobby. Within seconds they find themselves in full flow and their nerves have all but disappeared. The same is true of selling; when you know your topic—in this case your product, service, company, and industry—and when you are truly passionate about it, that passion is going to be obvious to your prospects and customers. And that in itself is a powerful selling technique, one that is underestimated by the vast majority of salespeople.

When we say knowledge is power, we are not only talking about the knowledge you as a salesperson possess, but also the knowledge consumers have in today's world. Go back thirty years and the sales environment was very different. Prior to the internet, most buyers had limited access to up-to-date information. They couldn't compare products without going to a store or consulting a technical specifications sheet (after waiting for it to arrive in the mail) or calling a manufacturer for a brochure—or perhaps, heaven forbid, spending hours at the local library. Price comparisons were extremely difficult to make back then, and real-time reviews were science fiction. Today, however, a shopper can not only compare the prices at stores in their area by going online, but they can also read product reviews. Online buying has thrown another huge wrench into the sales proposition—consumers can now purchase anything they want from their electronic device and have it delivered to their door in short order. It's never been more important to be able to offer something that is not so readily available from an online retailer or wholesaler, and that something is expert advice.

> ∨ *Online buying has thrown another huge wrench into*
> ∨ *the sales proposition—consumers can now purchase*
> ∨ *anything they want from their electronic device and*
> ∨ *have it delivered to their door in short order. It's never*
> ∨ *been more important to be able to offer something*
> ∨ *that is not so readily available from an online retailer*
> ∨ *or wholesaler, and that something is expert advice.*

The question you need to ask yourself is, who now has the power? To be successful in sales today, you have to manage information effectively and get the right information to the right people at the right time. You also have to provide more and better information; you have to show a level of expertise that exceeds that of the person to whom you are selling and, more importantly, that which is readily accessible online.

Consumers are constantly bombarded by information; after all, we live in the information age. As a result, consumers have become increasingly knowledgeable about what they are considering buying and from whom. No longer can salespeople bluff their way through a sales presentation; it is more than likely that the buyer will be better informed than the salesperson. Consider the fact that the salesperson's market, product, or service is constantly changing, as are the needs of their customers, and the power of information and knowledge becomes apparent. Salespeople need to be a beacon of consistency amid all this change and be a resource to their customers. Bottom line, you should be the person the prospect or customer trusts and turns to when they need information or assistance.

The power of knowledge lies in its ability to improve confidence and promote better communication between a customer and the salesperson, which in turn improves their relationship. In the case of the salesperson, knowledge and expertise bestows a perceived expert status that increases credibility. Great credibility comes from having enough verifiable knowledge to prove what you are saying.

Here's a rhetorical question: Would you prefer to purchase something from someone who is full of BS or from someone who is an expert? Salespeople who demonstrate superior knowledge can adopt a consultancy role. Anytime you are perceived as more of an advisor than a salesperson you are winning. Hi-Touch Selling occurs when all of the above happens and you are seen by customers as being an invaluable resource. At that point, in the eyes of the customer you move from offering an objective view of the product or service you are selling to a subjective one. And that is pure gold.

The good news is that most salespeople, even successful ones, have only a small fraction of the information and knowledge they could have to help them sell more. This means you have an opportunity to put your competition at a serious disadvantage.

In the previous section of this book, we discussed the importance of being committed; once you've made that leap, the next step is to become an expert. Let's explore that further and break down the various areas of knowledge that will separate you from other salespeople and make you a Hi-Touch super-salesperson. Make no mistake, knowledge IS power, and experts sell more—period.

How Not to Sell

- Who cares if you are an expert in your market and industry? You can always BS.
- Knowing your stuff doesn't make you a better salesperson.
- Knowledge has nothing to do with confidence. You can know nothing about what you are selling and fake confidence.
- Having more information than your prospects or customers doesn't give you any power, nor does it increase your credibility or give buyers greater trust in you.

SEVENTEEN

I Know What Industry I'm in; That's Enough

The degree to which you counter negative perceptions about your industry is the degree to which you will stand out from your competition. If you want to be at the top of your game, you need to know and understand the industry in which you operate. Each industry is complex and unique. Understanding the political, economic, technological, and market factors that influence yours will allow you to understand how it's developing, where it's heading, and what that means for you, your company, and your customers. In the mid-to-late 1990s, many people in the typesetting business got sideswiped when consumers and businesses started designing page layouts on their computers. Almost overnight the "paste-up" (phototypesetting) went the way of the dodo bird.

Salespeople who didn't see this coming ended up having to change companies and even careers, but not before they started to see their sales decline quickly, along with their commissions, of course.

⌄ *Each industry is complex and unique. Understanding*
⌄ *the political, economic, technological, and market*
⌄ *factors that influence yours will allow you to understand*
⌄ *how it's developing, where it's heading, and what that*
⌄ *means for you, your company, and your customers.*

One great way NOT to sell is to put your head in the sand and ignore the industry in which you operate. At least you'll never see the bullet train coming! Instead, ask yourself, "what industry am I in, and what's happening in it at the moment? What are the industry pundits saying, and is any of it important to me or my customers?" New technology, new products, new competition, and incoming or changing government regulations should all be areas of special interest. It's a good idea to subscribe to any and all trade magazines and follow the news. There is a goldmine of information contained between the pages of these publications, information that will make you look like an expert not only to your customers but also to your boss—keep up and succeed or ignore it at your peril.

How Not to Sell

- Industry knowledge is not important. Your company will provide you with all of the information you need to know.
- If regulations that affect your customers change or are introduced, that's their problem, not yours.
- Reading trade journals is so boring; they're just for know-it-alls and nerds.

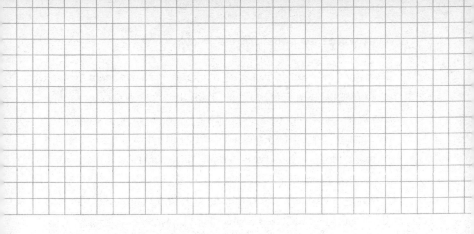

EIGHTEEN

Knowing My Local Market Is Not Important

Okay, so you know what's happening in your industry: now it's time to get local and think about the specific market in which you operate. This could be your territory, your specific niche, or a certain demographic. Your market is the environment in which your direct customers exist. Knowing what is happening with their local economy, local government, and anything else that has a bearing on what you sell and how you sell it is vital to your long-term security.

TYLER STARTED A pedicab business in a popular tourist town and had the market to himself for many years. He thought he was invincible; he even cut back his marketing to a minimum and still his business grew year-on-year. Tyler thought he was set for life. His business challenges were small and manageable, mostly related to finding strong-legged individuals who were reliable and had the right personality to deal with the tourists who frequented his city year-round.

Then, seemingly overnight, everything changed. Tyler had been living in a bubble; he never kept up with advances in his industry and paid little attention to his indirect competition, let alone any direct competition trying to enter his market. He thought he had his market completely sewn up. Unbeknown to him, another company had just relocated to his city, and the new kid on the block had a fleet of solar-powered eco rickshaws.

It took less than three months for them to decimate Tyler's business. His experienced and knowledgeable employees quickly moved to his competitor. After all, the solar-powered rickshaws made things easier going up hills or at the end of a particularly long day. Tourists loved the look of the rickshaws and appreciated the green aspect of the business. Tyler was already a relic of the past, and soon he was drastically cutting back and not long after that he was forced to close his business.

TYLER WAS NOT a salesperson for a company, but he was the primary salesperson for his business and he took his eye off the ball big-time.

How much do you know about your competition? Do you know what products they sell and how they compare with yours? How can you sell your strengths against their weaknesses? Are your prices higher or lower, and what does this mean when you factor in quality and value?

Have you researched which companies could potentially buy what you sell, or are you simply servicing the market you have or that you have inherited? How much of the market have you penetrated and what percentage do you currently control? You may well be surprised by what you're missing.

Studying local media outlets and publications can be extremely useful and give you a head start when it comes to new companies that are opening in or relocating to your area. Networking locally also gives you an opportunity to gain inside knowledge that can give you a leg up on your competition. John Naisbitt, in his book *Megatrends*, said that every town is run by one hundred people, no matter its size[1]—a good question to ask yourself is, how many of the one hundred power figures in your town do you know?

How Not to Sell

- Don't research your industry, market, prospects, or competition, and don't find out more about the features, advantages, and benefits of your product; it's a waste of time. All you need is charm and a good, strong, pushy sales technique.
- Your competition isn't a threat. What you sell is superior and who cares if they are having a special promotion?
- Don't worry about newcomers trying to steal your business—you're well-established, and they'll never be able to unseat you.

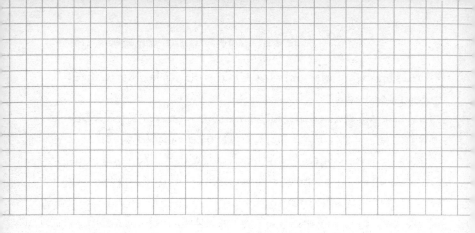

NINETEEN

Keep Business and Personal Stuff Separate

No one can sell in isolation; a relationship has to exist between the purchaser and the salesperson, and at least from the salesperson's perspective, that relationship can only succeed if it is based on more than a cursory knowledge of the customer.

ELIZABETH WORKED FOR a company selling commercial lighting; she covered a large territory and had almost a hundred customers that she maintained regularly. She was an analytical type and not prone to sharing personal information with her buyers. To her, business was business and she neither wanted to know anything about her customers' lives nor did she want them to know anything about hers. The problem was that she took this a little too literally and knew almost nothing about the people to whom she owed her livelihood.

One day she was in a coffee shop and came across several other reps who serviced many of the same customers that she did. They were gathered around a table and they invited her to join them. She was pleased; they were well-liked by some of her largest accounts and she knew they sold more than she did. She wanted to know how they had established such good relationships. As she listened to the conversation, she was amazed by how much they knew about her customers. It was like another world opened up and she began to see her customers in a whole new light. She discovered that one customer, whom she had found it very difficult to connect with lately, had recently lost his wife to cancer. Another she learned was just about to be promoted and would be heading up a division she had been trying to make inroads into for years.

As the gossip continued, she realized she knew very little about any of her accounts and it suddenly dawned on her that this was why her competitors were outselling her. Over the next several months she opened up a little when interacting with her buyers and they in turn started to share more about both their work and personal lives. She recalls that she started enjoying her job more, especially the increased commissions that resulted from a gradual but significant increase in her territory's revenues.

THE FACT IS, the more you know and understand about your customer and their needs, aspirations, and circumstances, the more likely it is that your relationship will be built on a solid and lasting foundation. Building a knowledge bank on your buyer is money, well . . . in the bank (cliché intended). Ask yourself, do you know how long they have been with the company, what they did prior to their current job, and what ambitions they have for the future? Do you know their hobbies and interests and whether they are single, married, or have children? Do you know their birthday?

> ∨   *Building a knowledge bank on your buyer is money,*
> ∨   *well . . . in the bank (cliché intended). Ask yourself, do*
> ∨   *you know how long they have been with the company,*
> ∨   *what they did prior to their current job, and what*
> ∨   *ambitions they have for the future?*

Of course, giving a customer or prospect the third degree won't go over well, but much of this information can be garnered from the exchange of a few pleasantries and an observant eye. You might find photographs of children or grandchildren on their desk perhaps, or framed graduation certificates on the wall, or a wedding band on their finger—a few thoughtful questions showing genuine interest might work wonders for your relationship. Simply asking a customer about their weekend can result in them sharing stories about a camping trip or their grandkids' lacrosse tournament, and thus you start to learn about their passions and start to build up their profile. Saying "happy birthday"—on the correct day, of course—is one of the most powerful ways for a salesperson to bond with a customer. Now that you know each other on a more friendly and personal basis, it will be easier to probe their needs and wants and discover how satisfied they are—or aren't—with their current suppliers.

All the while you should be identifying their social or behavioral style, as discussed in Chapter Two. Knowing this will allow you to be the person they want to deal with, the salesperson with whom they feel most comfortable, and the salesperson whose pitch they best understand. People buy from people they like—like them and get them to like you.

∨ *People buy from people they like—like them and*
∨ *get them to like you.*

How Not to Sell

- You don't need to know much about prospects. They're all the same: a potential commission.
- Knowing your customer's birthday, or that their spouse has been seriously ill recently, is weird. They'll think you are stalking them or something.
- Getting to know your customers won't give you an advantage over the competition. Business and personal matters should be kept strictly separate—heck, that might lead to being on a first-name basis and where will that end?

TWENTY

I Don't Need to Understand My Customer's Business

Although selling is more about relating to people than anything else, it's also about being professional and understanding the business world and more specifically your customer's business. What do you know about their company? Is it family owned and operated? Is it part of a franchise? Is there a big corporation behind the local façade? Knowing the answers to these questions can lead to further opportunities through recommendations, and it can also give you access to other levels of their business. How much do you know about the company's management structure? Do you know the decision-makers and owners?

ᐯ   *Although selling is more about relating to people than*
ᐯ   *anything else, it's also about being professional and*
ᐯ   *understanding the business world and more specifically*
ᐯ   *your customer's business.*

How are the company's finances? If they are a public company, have you researched their financial situation and read their annual report? You never know, they could be planning to expand and by knowing that nugget of information you might be able to beat your competition to a major sale to their new division, or for their new location.

CELIA WORKED AS a sales rep for a custom millwork company in a midsized town. Competition was tough, but her company was well respected, so they were holding their own. Her boss, Ian, was always onto her about keeping an eye out for ways to grow their business with existing customers. He networked heavily and the company was a member of several trade associations; Ian was also on the board of the local chamber of commerce.

Celia, however, was a special breed of salesperson. She preferred cold calling and bringing in new business and she was good at it; closing deals had never been an issue. She loved the hunt for new clients and in part that's why Ian had hired her initially. Schmoozing with the old guard wasn't her style and it was an ongoing issue between her and Ian that she felt there was little value to keeping in touch with or following up on previous customers. In her opinion, once they had done a major millwork job, the likelihood that the company would need anything significant from them in the future was low.

At their monthly sales meeting, Ian and Celia had once again argued their opposing views as to an effective sales strategy for Celia's territory. Ian had asked how many old customers she'd made contact with the previous month, eliciting Celia's reply that it was a waste of time and that, in that same period, she had brought in $80,000 of business from brand-new customers. Ian then asked her if she knew that the local Porsche dealership, an old customer for whom they had designed and built a showroom, was planning to open the first Maserati dealership in the state. This was the first Celia had heard of it; there had been no announcements in the local newspaper, and no one was talking about it, so how the heck did Ian know?

Celia hated the smug way Ian had made the announcement and she was feeling a mix of frustration, anger, and embarrassment. This got a whole lot worse when Ian passed her a document; it was a contract for the design and build-out of the new dealership worth a little over a half-million dollars. Ian let the silence hang for a moment or two and said, "So there's little to no value in keeping in touch with old customers, eh?"

THERE IS ALMOST no possible scenario where knowing less about your customer is a positive, and the only scenarios that do come to mind could not be repeated here. As we mentioned earlier, how you apply the knowledge you gain is going to have a bearing on its usefulness and value.

How Not to Sell

- All companies are the same, so don't bother doing any background research into your prospects or customers.
- There's little point in keeping in touch with old customers: focus on building your territory or business by going after new business.
- Previous customers know you; they'll come to you if they need something, so there's no need to pester them.
- Your job is to sell things, not foster ongoing relationships with customers.

TWENTY-ONE

My Employer's Business Is None of Mine

We talked earlier about the importance of being committed to your company, and how that commitment puts you in a positive light with buyers. Knowing everything about your company amps that commitment up a few notches. Salespeople who are a fan of the company they work for, who are aware when it is mentioned in the media, and who know about new products or technology well in advance of their release will always win out. The salesperson who knows and has a solid relationship with the highest number of people in their company usually sells more.

IF THAT SOUNDS far-fetched consider Jen; Jen works in the sales department at a refrigeration company. She is friendly with the entire sales team and all its support staff, and she is also on a first-name basis with the head of marketing, the sales director, and the accounts manager—in fact, she knows everyone in the firm that has any connection or relationship with her customers. In this way she can ensure her customers get first-class support from the head office regarding anything, from marketing opportunities to special offers; if and when there is any issue with their account, she can make sure it's dealt with promptly. The ability to "pull strings" to help your customers inevitably leads to happier accounts and more regular, and potentially larger, orders.

Her colleague Brandon, on the other hand, continually complains that Jen is the company's favorite and that she always gets to know about specials sooner than he does and she's always offered the plum new accounts.

JEN AND BRANDON work for the same company but are experiencing very different levels of support. Guess who's more often at the top in sales each month and who is usually toward the bottom?

Knowing what is going on within and around your company can also affect your credibility. Let's take a look at Ryan, for instance, who works for a janitorial services company.

RYAN WAS COMPLETELY baffled when a customer asked how he felt about his company being bought out by their primary competitor. This was bad on so many levels—not only did he look out of touch (not to mention stupid) in front of his customer, but he was now unsure of his standing with the company. One can only imagine what the customer thought of the stunned look on his face. The fact that his customer knew meant that the buyout was at least semi-public knowledge. The fact that Ryan was oblivious to what was going on within his own company meant he probably had a lot more to be concerned about than simply losing credibility with his customer.

RYAN COULD HAVE set up an alert with Google or another browser to notify him of any news relating to his company. He also could have, quite simply, frequented the office more, or called in regularly to make sure that he was in the loop. As mentioned earlier, never underestimate the person at the front desk who answers the phones; he or she operates at the hub of the company and knows where all the bodies are buried. Make friends with them and they will watch your back—at least until they watch you walking out the door for the last time!

The more you know about your company and the more you understand its ownership, top management, mission, and philosophies—even its stance on the environment—the more valuable you become, not only to the management but also to your customers.

How Not to Sell

- Keep a low profile and only go into the office when you really need to.
- Ignore the front-desk person—they don't know anything about sales.
- Never visit the finance department; remember, your job is sales not money.

TWENTY-TWO

If a Customer Needs Product Information, They Can Visit Our Website

It's a very old example but worth repeating: when someone buys a drill bit, they don't actually want a drill bit. They want a hole. There is power in understanding exactly what it is that your customer wants and needs. Consider how wanting a hole but needing a drill applies to your world. Think about how what you sell benefits your customers—what are the features, advantages, and benefits of your products and services, and what problems or needs do they answer? Look at how they stack up against the competition, at strengths and weaknesses on both sides of the equation. Is there any way in which your product or service is unique? Does it have a USP (unique selling proposition), and if so what is it?

⌄   *There is power in understanding exactly what it is that*
⌄   *your customer wants and needs.*

The curveball in all of this is that people see things differently according to their behavioral or social style, as we discussed way back in Chapter Five. An Analytical will be interested in the technical specifications of what you sell—the details. The Expressive will be interested in the look-good, feel-good factor, while your Amiable customer is going to want to feel protected and safe. Then there's the Driver who wants whatever you sell to make them money and save them time, and they want it fast.

Looking back at Sheila and her car purchase, it's clear that she was interested in safety first. Her husband, however, would have wanted something flashy—he would have prioritized design along with the ability to drive fast. Yep, you guessed it: Mike is an Expressive. Safe, reliable, hard-wearing cars, on the other hand, are driven by Analyticals and Amiables. Luxury, prestigious cars with a high resale value are most frequently purchased by people exhibiting a Driven behavioral style.

Knowing as much as you can about your products or services, and understanding them in finite detail, is one of the most powerful weapons you can have in your sales arsenal—it's how TO sell and sell well!

How Not to Sell

- All customers have the same perspective on what you're selling and how you sell it.
- Don't spend too much time getting to know the features, advantages, and benefits of your product or service. Your prospect can read the sales literature themselves, or visit your company's website.
- Don't try to figure out what's unique about what you are selling; prospects only care about price.

TWENTY-THREE

Planning? I'm Better at Just Winging It

Many salespeople simply head out to meet with prospects or call them with no plan in place. This chapter will discuss the value of creating a sales plan that also includes a sales process. There is great value in setting expectations prior to a sales call. For instance, not all calls are likely to result in an order on the first visit, so what *is* your expectation?

Selling is not always about getting the sale. Too often, salespeople get hung up on making a sale every time they interact with a prospect or an existing customer. That's crazy. If the call is your first contact with a prospect, it's unlikely, although not impossible, you will get a sale. Here's a story from a sales manager about a salesperson whose expectations were out of whack.

EMILY WORKED FOR an insurance company and was heading into a meeting with a stockbroker to discuss a healthcare plan for his small businesses. Accompanying her was Jess, her direct report. Jess was there because Emily was in a slump and needed help. Emily was desperate for a sale and had lost sight of what she wanted to happen in the meeting she was about to enter. As they were about to knock on the prospect's door, Emily said, "I better make this sale. My numbers are so down, this guy better not mess with me." At that moment Jess stopped Emily from knocking on the door and said, "Whoa! Wait a minute, if your focus is solely on making the sale, or hitting your numbers, that's exactly what you're NOT going to achieve. That stockbroker in there doesn't care about your goals or your targets or all the bills you have to pay. They will say 'no' every time to that. Think about how you can help him instead. You have one chance to make a first impression and whatever you're thinking or feeling right before you walk in the door is the impression you're going to give your client. Focus on helping him and you'll get what you need, too."

Emily took a deep breath, sighed, and remembered that, in the past, she had to be told this same advice, but she'd never been lucky enough to have someone catch her in the moment. She knew what she had to do; focus less on getting the sale and more on meeting her customer's needs.

TAKE A STEP back and ask yourself, "What do I want to happen at this meeting? What outcome can I realistically expect?" Focus on realistic expectations, which could run the gamut from a highly optimistic "get a big sale" to "get the prospect to agree to allow me to put a quote together" to "get a follow-up meeting where all the decision-makers will be present."

The sales process is just that, a process, and sometimes it's complex. Jess, Emily's boss in the story above, sums it up well: "Sales motivation is so focused on the salesperson reaching their goals that they forget that their income is only a by-product of the number of people whose problems they helped solve. Focus on that and selling becomes easy, genuine, and authentic. You'll far surpass those who are just trying to reach their monthly quotas."

- ⌄ *Sales motivation is so focused on the salesperson*
- ⌄ *reaching their goals that they forget that their income*
- ⌄ *is only a by-product of the number of people whose*
- ⌄ *problems they helped solve. Focus on that and selling*
- ⌄ *becomes easy, genuine, and authentic. You'll far*
- ⌄ *surpass those who are just trying to reach their*
- ⌄ *monthly quotas.*

A sales process for a new product, new market, or new business could be as simple as:

- Choose the target market.
- Create a prospect list.
- Research the companies on your prospect list.
- Send an email or a letter (or cold call).
- Follow up by telephone.
- Identify the decision-maker(s).
- Qualify the buyer/decision-maker.
- Identify the prospect's decision-making process.

- Arrange a meeting.
- Make your presentation.
- Make the sale or arrange a follow-up meeting.

Having a sales strategy allows you to identify what outcome you want from each stage of the process. If you are still in discovery mode—that is, trying to identify who you should be selling to—"make the sale" wouldn't be a good goal. However, something like, "identify the decision-maker, ascertain their initial interest, and make an appointment to meet with them," might be.

Once you have an appointment with a real, live person, then you can consider the outcome you want from the meeting. Obviously, every salesperson wants to make the sale at the earliest opportunity but think hard about every interaction and be prepared to alter your expectations as the meeting unfolds. Car salespersons often try to force a sale immediately; by doing so they alienate buyers who might be in the early stages of making a decision about the make and model of the car they want to purchase. A better expectation would be to make the prospective buyer feel comfortable at the dealership, and build credibility and trust so that even if they visit other dealers, they end up *wanting* to do business with you.

A B2B sales representative might set their list of objectives at an initial meeting as: ascertain my client's needs, discover their budget and their buying process, qualify the buyer, identify what products they have used in the past, ask who else they are considering as a supplier, and maybe also ask about my client's timeline. Their goal for the meeting might be to set the date for the delivery of a proposal, estimate, or quote, or to return and make a presentation.

By knowing what you want and expect to happen at a meeting, you are far more likely to be able to focus on getting the job done than if you go in not knowing what to expect and hoping for the best. Preplanning calls is what sales professionals do—at least the ones who make six-figure incomes.

How Not to Sell

- Never plan a call—just wing it. It's nice to be surprised once in a while.
- Don't set expectations. They are too much like targets—also, why be disappointed?
- Expect every interaction with a prospect or buyer to end in a sale. If it doesn't, you've failed.
- The goal is always to come out with a sale, no matter what.
- It's not about you helping customers reach their goals: it's about them helping you reach your goals.
- Selling is easy; find a prospect, talk to them, pitch them, sell them, earn your commission, and move on as fast as you can.
- Only weak salespeople need a strategy.

TWENTY-FOUR

I Don't Have Time for Paperwork

Many salespeople enjoy selling but hate doing paperwork; however, it goes with the territory (pun intended). Handling the business side of selling is vital to success. Salespeople who are entrepreneurial employees are far more successful because they take ownership and run their territory like it's their own small business. And, in a way, it is—think about it for a moment. You have responsibility for an operating unit. You need to make your territory profitable by prospecting and making sales. You may also be responsible to some degree for marketing and promotions. Just like any business owner or entrepreneur, you have targets. Highly successful salespeople are the ones who put the time in to do the admin part of the job. But what does all that paperwork involve? A lot depends on the type of selling you are doing and the sophistication of your company's sales operation, but here's some of the paperwork "stuff" that might help you become a top performer.

> ∨ *Highly successful salespeople are the ones who put the*
> ∨ *time in to do the admin part of the job. But what does*
> ∨ *all that paperwork involve? A lot depends on the type*
> ∨ *of selling you are doing and the sophistication of your*
> ∨ *company's sales operation.*

If you want to be a true professional, then you might want to use a CRM (Customer Relationship Management) system. Many corporations use a system like this, which allows them to manage their entire customer relationship through the systemized collection and utilization of information. This ranges from collecting tombstone data to tracking every salesperson/customer interaction. CRMs allow salespeople to store contact and account information in a central location. This information can include everything from ordering details to product preferences to buyer background and history—just about anything that might be useful to the account's current sales rep and, importantly, to their successors.

This information is accessible in real time (assuming it is stored in the cloud) by anyone with permission. However, make no mistake, CRM is not solely a prerogative for major corporations—individual salespeople can use it to make themselves considerably more efficient. One important point is that although commercial CRM systems make life easier, there is no reason why you can't collate all this information simply in a program such as Microsoft Excel, or even Microsoft Word using tables.

The key to CRM is its ability to build an intimate picture of your relationship with both your prospects and your customers. However, if formal CRM software is a little too high tech or outside of your budget, you can collect the information yourself. You should track what occurred during every meeting to build a detailed picture of your client over time. After every meeting or phone call note when it took place, whom it was with, what decisions were made, what questions were asked, what requests made, what orders taken, the date and time of your next appointment, and any personal information you might have learned—that includes birthdays, house or business moves, past promotions and successes, and the birth of a child or grandchild. Absolutely anything can and could be relevant at some stage.

Paperwork is part and parcel of the professional sales process; it separates those that have a short-term approach from those who are taking sales seriously and are in it for the long haul. Often, salespeople have a "sell once and move on" philosophy. It's particularly characteristic of automobile salespeople—staff turnover at car dealerships is exceptionally high. If you want to take the long-haul approach to your sales career, carefully maintained paperwork is the secret ingredient that will allow you to exponentially grow your business, your territory, and your reputation. It's obvious when you think about it, but let's drop in on Brett, who sells furniture at a retail outlet.

BRETT WORKS FOR a high-turnover, low-price, medium-quality furniture warehouse. He's been trained to greet customers as they walk through the door and to engage them in banal banter while following them around the store. Even when they are obviously uncomfortable, Brett sticks with them, although he does increase his distance from them. Several are so uncomfortable they make their way to the door and exit without seriously looking at anything. When Brett does get a sale, he does the minimum amount of paperwork his company insists on, which is basically tombstone data, delivery details, and of course payment information. As soon as this is complete, he moves on to stalk his next victim. Within six months, Brett is no longer with the company and is selling burial plots—the all-time dead-end job.

APOLOGIES FOR THE pun and to anyone selling burial plots, but the analogy was too good to pass over. Brett is not committed to his job, his product, or his customer; he is committed to making a quick and easy buck. The problem is that this will never happen so long as he continues to use this strategy. Ashley, on the other hand—who works for a crosstown furniture warehouse—has a different sales approach:

ASHLEY ALSO WELCOMES people as they enter the store. She hands customers her business card and tells them she will be happy to answer any questions they might have, but for now, they should feel free to wander the store at their leisure.

A couple walks into the store and when Ashley introduces herself, she makes sure she gets their names: Rachel and Logan. She also makes a few comments about the weather, compliments Rachel on what she is wearing, and asks if they are looking for anything in particular. She is relaxed and exerts zero pressure.

She then moves to a central location in the store where she can be easily seen. At that point she makes a few notes about the people she just greeted. Her notes might read a little like this: "Young couple, Logan and Rachel: late twenties, live local, well dressed, possibly looking for a coffee table for their condo. She looks as if she might be pregnant. He is outgoing, clean hands, well-groomed, probably works in an office, maybe high tech. She's well-dressed, well-spoken, and fairly reserved—government or not-for-profit worker? Logan's likely an Expressive and Rachel's an Amiable. Long-term potential."

A little later, the couple comes up to Ashley and asks a few questions about coffee tables and Ashley makes the sale. But before she writes it up, she asks if they saw that there was a sale on table lamps and ends up selling them a lamp, too. When she finally writes up the order, she chats with them and starts to build a relationship. She is careful to include Rachel in the conversation, as she knows it would be easy to fall into the trap of speaking solely to Logan, who is chatty and fun. By the time Logan and Rachel leave, Ashely has gathered a lot of information about their future plans and discovers they are getting married soon and moving into their first home together. She asks them if she can occasionally email them to let them know about special offers at the store. She has also discovered Rachel's due date and the fact they are both big fans of country music. Ashley creates a personal file on the couple and stores it with the fifty or so others she has created over the past few months. The following day she sends them a thank-you card.

Five weeks later, she stumbles upon the fact that Jason Aldean has announced an unexpected appearance at a nearby summer country music festival. Ashley emails Logan and Rachel with the news, linking to a site where they can buy tickets, and takes the opportunity to ask them how they're doing. Rachel emails back thanking Ashley and says they are fine and plan to move into their new home the following month. Ashley makes a note of this and shortly after she knows they have moved she sends them a card congratulating them on their new home and includes a discount coupon.

To cut a long story—not to mention a long relationship—short, Rachel and Logan became regular customers and relied heavily on Ashley's advice when furnishing their new home. Fast-forward ten years, and Ashley's list of what she has sold the couple is long. They now have three children, so over the years they have come back to purchase three kids' beds and a ton of other stuff, including sofas, a dining room table, and chairs.

Ashley is now the store manager and her client file (the paperwork) is kept in a three-ring binder. She has been invited to four parties at Rachel and Logan's house, where she has met many new customers. Over the years she has gotten to know them very well and she sends them birthday and wedding anniversary cards, touching base whenever she hears about an event she thinks they might be interested in attending. For their part, Rachel and Logan would never think of buying from any other store.

THIS IS JUST one example of how to make "paperwork" count. It doesn't matter if you work in B2B, or a B2C environment like Ashley: keeping records, knowing your customers, and tracking sales pays off, unless you prefer to be like Brett and are happy to keep reinventing the wheel.

How Not to Sell

- Paperwork is a waste of time; just take the orders and hand them in. It's not important to record information like the date of the sale, the buyer's name, or where and how they want your product delivered.
- Don't worry, in a B2C environment customers are like buses. Another one will be along soon.
- Customers are never loyal, so it's pointless to try to get to know them.
- Keeping records takes time away from selling. Focus on selling to fresh meat.
- In a B2B environment, don't keep customer records—staff change all the time. Just ask to see the "buyer" on your next visit, and they'll know who you mean. And who cares if it's their birthday—what's that to you?

Section 3

It's All
about the Sale

The only thing standing in the way of a sale is an objection.
Once there are no objections you have the sale.   —Mike Wicks[1]

In this section we take a deep dive into the act of selling, from making sales presentations to handling objections to closing sales and following up with customers. We discuss some of the biggest mistakes salespeople make, including not handling objections appropriately, not asking for an order, and failing to follow up. This is fertile ground for our how-not-to-sell theme. Salespeople the world over seem to find every way possible to screw up getting the order, when in reality closing a sale is the natural conclusion to a positive interaction between those with a need and those with something that can satisfy that need at a price the prospect can afford to pay. Oh, if it were really that simple.

TWENTY-FIVE

A Good Pitch Is One Where No One Interrupts Me

Prospects can spot a slick sales pitch from a mile away; sales presentations need to be delivered in an inclusive, interactive fashion and not as a product, or salesperson's ego trip. In this chapter we'll offer tips and advice on how to make a sales presentation interesting and effective. We'll also talk about negotiation, active listening, and other dos and don'ts relevant to effectively being "onstage."

Kent describes a sales presentation from hell and exposes how incredibly bad they can be, along with the tricks of the trade that are utilized to get you to say yes; in this case at a sales pitch for private residences in Mexico. His experience was similar to those who have been trapped in a timeshare sales pitch. Kent's story of a ninety-minute presentation that turned into a five-hour shake-down is a great example of how not to sell.

UPON ARRIVING IN Puerto Vallarta, my wife and I took a shuttle to the rental car company where we made small talk with one of the employees (or at least that was what we thought we were doing). He asked if we had plans and if we'd be interested in a dolphin adventure. He said he would give us two tickets for free if we sat through a sales presentation at a local resort. To sweeten the deal, he promised a fancy buffet lunch and $200 cash upon completing the tour. We agreed, paid a refundable deposit, and met up with his colleague outside our rental unit to be guided to the resort.

The resort was one of a collection of private residence communities. We signed in with another couple who had also been enticed to attend by the promise of swimming with dolphins and were escorted to a dining hall where our sales rep, whom we'll call Chuck, asked us a few questions. He then walked us to a buffet and delivered on the promise of an excellent meal, demonstrating what those living in the community enjoyed every day. Little did we know it would be nearly five hours before we were able to leave, and by that time, we all felt like we'd lost an entire vacation day.

Once my wife and I gave a firm no, the salesman went from personable family man to desperate salesman on the verge of losing his job. He became a pouting child who refused to shake hands and say goodbye. The whole experience was frustrating, sad, and ineffective.

THERE ARE SO many things wrong with sales presentations like this that it's hard to know where to start. In the first three chapters, we discussed the importance of qualifying your prospects before starting to sell to them; in the type of selling described above, bribery is used to get just about anyone to listen to a sales pitch. These salespeople want to make prospects feel obligated to sit through the full sales presentation; in this case a bait (ninety minutes) and switch (five hours). They also put prospects into a position where they feel they are going to lose something if they leave before the salesperson has finished. The vast majority of people in this situation feel uncomfortable, which manifests itself as anger, frustration, or ultimately resignation, none of which are conducive to making a sale. Even if the sale does happen, it will often result in buyer's remorse.

One of the many problems with this approach is that the qualifying process is done during the sales presentation itself when those prospects who might be interested are sitting alongside those that are getting frustrated and trying to escape. The fact that Kent was promised a ninety-minute presentation that morphed into a vigorous five-hour sales pitch is another example of how not to sell; a salesperson should never break promises. Think about it for a moment—can you trust a person who can't keep their promises? Of course not.

Sales presentations such as the one Kent describes are almost always one-way: points are made, promises are given, the product is described, and easy payments are outlined; the only requisite interaction is that the prospects have to continually agree with everything that is being presented. They "get them used to saying yes." As we will see in the next chapter, these presentations are designed to prevent prospects from coming up with objections.

Finally, salespeople using the "timeshare" approach take their prospects, or perhaps a better word might be victims, on a roller-coaster ride of emotions. As Kent says, their salesperson went from friendly to desperate to sulky in short order. In many ways he was fortunate as salespeople in this line of business can often become angry and accuse prospects of wasting their time. In reality, the reverse is true, but it's all about manipulating emotions.

The reason this sales approach is still used is that, as we have said before, sales is often a numbers game and eventually these salespeople will catch someone who is either genuinely interested in making such a purchase or who can be convinced that it's a good idea. Conversion rates are quite low, but if as a salesperson you have extremely limited sales skills you need a continual large intake of prospects.

Leaving the somewhat shady world of resort and timeshare selling behind, even a salesperson who does almost everything right can fail by being a little too committed to his or her sales presentation.

Samantha is a sales rep selling video games to retailers across a large territory. Here, she recalls for us when she was an eighteen-year-old trainee giving a presentation to the manager of a larger store in front of her sales trainer. She was selling a new car racing game and James, whose territory they were on, had told her he expected a good order for this major new game.

I'D DONE MY homework and knew all about every game I was about to present. I was as confident as an eighteen-year-old can be—I gave it all I had, and the buyer seemed positive. I told her everything I knew about a particular game; I even relayed some great background and technical information, which got her even more excited. I spent more time on our lead title than all the other games on our list that day. When I was finished, she gave me an order for one hundred copies. This was a good order—in my mind amazing—and I was pumped. As we left the store, James turned to me, gave me the keys to his car, and told me to wait for him.

When he returned, he reviewed my sales presentation. It was good overall, he said. He was impressed that I knew my products, especially the extra tidbits of information that had gotten such a good response from the buyer, and also that I came across as confident and enthusiastic but not pushy. The only trouble, he said, was that I had not spotted the buying signals and had talked so much about one game in particular that the buyer started having second thoughts about how many to order. Although the order for one hundred was good, I could have gotten a much larger one. Seeing the look of disbelief in my eyes, my trainer pulled out the order we had just received and showed me that when he went back into the store, he had managed to get the order raised to 250 copies. I was stunned.

WHAT SAMANTHA HAD not realized at that time was the importance of understanding the emotion that a buyer undergoes during the selling process. We'll go into this in a little more detail in the chapter on closing but suffice to say that during a good sales pitch a buyer will experience an emotional response to what's being said. If they like what they are seeing and hearing—and if the salesperson relays the product's features, advantages, and benefits accurately and enthusiastically—they will progressively (and silently) increase the number of products they might purchase. At a certain point, however, they will start to think more logically, and if the salesperson drones on for too long, doubts will creep in and the order quantity will start to fall.

> ∨   *During a good sales pitch a buyer will experience*
> ∨   *an emotional response to what's being said. If they*
> ∨   *like what they are seeing and hearing—and if the*
> ∨   *salesperson relays the product's features, advantages,*
> ∨   *and benefits accurately and enthusiastically—they will*
> ∨   *progressively (and silently) increase the number of*
> ∨   *products they might purchase.*

How Not to Sell

- If at all possible, trap your prospect so that they can't escape your sales pitch.
- Promise prospects a short presentation and once you have them captive keep them as long as it takes to get the sale.
- Make your sales pitch flashy and light on actual facts. Go for the sizzle not the steak. There's no need to do any detailed research—just rely on your personality.
- Make your sales pitch full of complex information, facts, and figures. Bamboozle the customer with details; they'll be impressed.
- Don't let anyone prevent you from finishing your sales pitch even if you think they might be ready to make a purchase; they'll probably order more by the time you finish.
- If it looks like you are going to lose the sale, it's okay to show your frustration and make the prospect feel guilty about wasting your time and losing your commission.

- Emphasize your company's experience and size; prospects aren't looking for features, advantages, benefits, and fresh ideas.

- Give people something to make them feel obliged to hear your sales pitch—making them feel guilty is a great way to get a sale.

- You don't need to answer questions; just tell prospects what they need.

- Listening is overrated; you just need to get all your points across as quickly and forcefully as possible before they ask any questions or bring up an objection.

- You can be a little loose with the facts; no one's going to check. Integrity is for losers and you have targets to meet (or do you?).

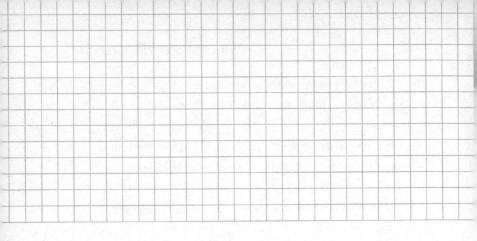

TWENTY-SIX

Formal Presentations Are Best Done Off the Cuff

Sales pitches and presentations come in all forms, the most formal being a full-blown audio-visual presentation. For the longest time, PowerPoint and Apple's equivalent, Keynote, were used to deliver this type of sales presentation and still are, although today there are many more sophisticated and "sexy" ways to make presentations; some reps even use AI (search best presentation software). Whichever medium you use, though, the principles of making a good sales presentation remain the same. Christopher, who works for an office furniture supplier, offers us a great example of how not to wow an audience of prospective buyers. This tale dates back a few years, but Christopher told us he still cringes when he remembers this presentation from hell early in his career.

HE WAS SCHEDULED to deliver a sales presentation to several department heads at a leading civil engineering and land development company who were looking to upgrade and replace their firm's office furniture. Christopher remembers being well briefed by his area manager on the points he needed to get across—they were his company's history, experience, credentials, and efficiency and its understanding of the trend toward increasing overall effectiveness, innovation, diverse thought, and creativity by having employees work in teams. He was to emphasize that most workplaces experience difficulty adapting to these changing needs, which require mobility and flexibility in the office environment, but at the same time assure the prospect that he and his company would be there with them every step of the way.

He was then supposed to present the products, technologies, and solutions that his company's technical team had designed specifically for them. In this phase of his presentation, his instructions were to highlight how his company had used the newest planning methodologies such as web-based survey tools to analyze how their employees worked to develop the unique package he was about to present. There were a bunch of other points he needed to cover, such as his company's green credentials and corporate sustainability initiatives, but you get the idea. What could go wrong?

He turned up at the prospect's offices only five minutes before his presentation was supposed to start; he'd had to pop back to his office because he'd forgotten his notes and parking had been difficult as usual. By the time he got to the their boardroom, he was hot, sweaty, and bordering on panic. It was all downhill from there. As promised, an electronic projector had been provided but it was a model he'd never seen before and he couldn't get the presentation on his laptop to make its way onto the projection screen. By now he was sweating profusely and wildly pressing any and every button on the state-of-the-art projector—all to no avail. To make things worse, his "audience" was starting to file into the room and take their seats and he was beginning to regret drinking that second cup of coffee earlier. Luckily, one of the managers helped him marry his laptop to the projector, and at last what was on his screen appeared on the boardroom wall. Unfortunately, it was his laptop's wallpaper, which was currently a photograph of him and his girlfriend on a beach in Hawaii wearing, well, not very much. Ignoring the smirks from everyone watching, he quickly managed to bring up the PowerPoint presentation he had prepared, and for the first time since he had arrived, he felt like he might be able to pull things back from the brink of disaster. He was wrong.

The final stragglers arrived and took their places around the boardroom table. Christopher introduced himself for the benefit of those who didn't know him and launched into his first slide, which contained ten bullet points outlining his company's history.

At this point we should remember that this was early in Christopher's career. He recalls that this was his first presentation to a major client and originally his area manager was going to accompany him, so what follows is at least in part excusable. However, as you read this, know that there are sales professionals everywhere making these same mistakes in offices and boardrooms across the country.

Instead of allowing the bullet points to speak for themselves, Christopher slowly starts to read them to the department heads in the room. Already he is losing them, and at least one is thinking, "Does he think we can't read?"

Christopher drones on and after seven slides he has yet to reach anything of particular interest to those present. His use of old-fashioned cartoonish clip art, which he thought was cute when he sprinkled it throughout the slides, has some rolling their eyes. Finally he gets into the main part of his sales presentation, where he has added photographs of the products his team is recommending; unfortunately, this has reduced the space available for copy, and the presentation is now using a 12-point font that has everyone squinting at the screen. The legibility issue is further exacerbated by the fact that Christopher felt it would be cool to use a fancy font called Brush Script. Eyes continue to glaze over.

Finally, he reaches the budget slide, of which he is particularly proud; he remembers spending hours earlier on the Excel spreadsheet that is now a blurry screen grab on the slide. As he takes his audience through the figures, he loses even those members who were still trying their best to learn what his company was offering them as a solution to their workplace challenges; challenges that were becoming greater by the minute.

CHRISTOPHER WAS NO doubt keen, but he failed to realize that making a sales presentation is still selling and most definitely not lecturing. Befriending the IT person responsible for ensuring a projector will be available is a golden rule for giving a good presentation; better still, rent or purchase your own. If you are using your client's equipment, arrive early with multiple dongles to ensure you can link your tablet or laptop to the projector without delay. Fifteen years ago, electronic projectors were heavy and cumbersome and prohibitively expensive for the average salesperson; today you can purchase pocket versions for under $300, which weigh less than one pound, and which are suitable for presenting to small groups.

Arriving early also gives you the opportunity to rearrange the room to suit your presentation style and allows you to set up any supplementary material you may wish to leave with your audience. If all of that doesn't convince you to arrive early then consider how good you will feel if you aren't hot, sweaty, and frantic and have enough time to do a quick run-through of your slides before the first person arrives. Heck, you may even have time to do a five-minute meditation.

Christopher, on the other hand, arrived late, lectured for forty-five minutes, and avoided taking any questions until the final slide had been painstakingly read to the department heads. He did almost everything wrong. Whole books have been written on making presentations, but here are ten tips to put you on the right track when it comes to wowing your audience.

1. Start with some relevant statistics or facts to catch your audience's attention. Ignore your colleagues' advice to tell a joke.
2. Don't linger too long on your company's credibility, experience, and history; the fact that you have decision-makers in the room means they already know you have the ability to deliver. A quick reminder is all that's necessary.
3. Early on in the presentation, tell your audience how you are going to help them solve their problems and challenges. Think of this as the "what's in it for me" statement. If Christopher had stated that he was going to solve their workplace challenges and make their company's

operations more efficient, he would have grabbed the room's attention from the outset.

4. Outline the challenges your customer faces—show that you have a grasp of their situation and the problems that need attention. Your audience needs to know you understand them before you can hope to convince them you have the answers they need.

5. Christopher would have been better having one message per slide; if several bulletpoints were required, they should have been short and in at least a 24-point (but preferably 30-point) Arial or Times New Roman font.

6. Christopher made the mistake of reading his slides, which is, frankly, insulting to the audience. Bullets help to keep both presenters and audience members on track but can be boring so if possible, use images in place of words where appropriate.

7. Keep any sales presentation short (to a maximum twenty minutes) and allow questions. Many experts say that after ten slides you begin to lose your audience, no matter the quality of your information.

8. If it's important to show a budget or pricing, never insert a screengrab or import an Excel spreadsheet. Using the largest typeface possible, extract the key figures you wish to discuss and use these on your slide. Then provide printed spreadsheets to your prospects so they can refer to the full document themselves if they wish to dig deeper.

9. Revisit the challenge, or pain, you are going to alleviate and demonstrate/justify the value of your solution.

10. Finally, leave your prospects with a vision of what their life will be like if they adopt your solution.

Reserve plenty of time for questions and expect objections. In Chapter Twenty-Nine we'll discuss why objections are a good thing and tell you how you can learn to love them.

More often than not, you will not be the only salesperson making a presentation. Your competition will also be trying their best to get your prospect's business. This will necessitate some advanced sales presentation techniques.

In the following story, we learn how Danielle and Steve handled being the underdogs when pitching for a major contract and in the end succeeded in beating the frontrunners, all due to their innovative sales presentations.

DANIELLE WAS CO-OWNER of a corporate sponsorship consulting firm that helped government and nonprofit organizations strategize on how to attract corporate sponsorships and monetize their assets. On this occasion the company was pitching a not-for-profit, quasi-government heritage organization. The organization had issued an RFP for an audit so they could ascertain their corporate sponsorship and fundraising potential. This was to be followed, under the same contract, by a comprehensive corporate sponsorship strategy, including advice on how to market its sites to potential sponsors. Danielle had managed to get on a shortlist of six companies that were under consideration for the contract. She had to present to a selection committee, which, over the course of a day-long marathon session, was to hear three presentations in the morning and three in the afternoon.

Danielle was the last to present, at 4 p.m. She knew she was better placed than at least three of the other companies but there was one firm that was significantly larger than hers and that also had excellent credentials; they were going to be tough to beat. Her business partner, Steve, suggested they try something a little different with their PowerPoint presentation, something that might make them stand out. Presenting last was a disadvantage, especially since they were unsure of when their biggest competition would be strutting their stuff, which they knew would be high-tech and impressive. Rather than try to compete with them head-on and deliver a slick presentation, they decided to go a different route.

Danielle and Steve worked hard in the days leading up to the presentation. Without a doubt they were taking a risk: Steve's idea was to turn the disadvantage of going last into an advantage by using a high-quality photograph of a heavily tree-lined lane as the background to the first and last slides, which were also set to classical music. The remaining slides would also display a faded-out pastoral scene featuring one of the properties under the organization's purview. The copy on the slides provided an overview of their company, its credentials, how they would approach delivering on the requirements outlined in the RFP, and why their approach would provide the financial results the organization needed.

On the day of the presentation, Danielle set up while the committee members were having coffee. When they returned and sat down, she gave them a minute to get settled and then started her presentation, saying nothing for thirty seconds while everyone in the room sat listening to a clarinet concerto and looking at the beautiful tree-lined lane and Danielle's company logo, discreetly placed in the bottom right-hand corner of the image. As the music faded out, she introduced herself and said, "After such a long day,

we thought you might like a few seconds of peace and contempla-
tion before listening to yet another presentation." Every single
person in the room smiled and nodded their approval.

Danielle had achieved her first objective, which was to be
memorable, and her second, which was to get the room's undi-
vided attention. She knew her second slide had fulfilled its pur-
pose when one of the members of the committee nudged his
colleague and pointed to the building in the photograph, recog-
nizing it as one of their properties. Late afternoon presentations
are typically made to a room of yawners, but not today: people
were awake, watching, and listening. She delivered all the key information clearly and concisely in six slides before anyone started
fidgeting and ended with what she hoped was the coup de grâce.
She had spent a lot of time with Steve coming up with a quote—
something that summed up the organization she was presenting
to; it wasn't that she expected them to adopt it as their new mission statement or anything—she just wanted to show them that
she understood their core values. So, when she came to the last
slide, she let the music play once again and let them read the
words, saying nothing for thirty seconds. Apart from the haunting
melody playing quietly in the background, you could have heard a
pin drop.

Once again there were smiles and nods before she asked if
there were any questions. One person commented that she had
obviously done her homework and the person with whom she had
already been in contact thanked her warmly. Steve handed out
color copies of the presentation, noticing that none of those present seemed to have any materials from the previous presenters.

DANIELLE AND STEVE'S story provides a good example of the thought and effort required when selling against stiff competition. They had been told that the winning company would be notified within seven days. When ten days had passed, they reached out to their contact to discover that the committee couldn't decide between Danielle's company and the company she had expected might win the contract. She was asked to make another presentation head-to-head with the other company in a few weeks' time. As the contract was worth many tens of thousands of dollars and could lead to further business with the organization, she agreed. They discovered that this time they were to present first, with their competition immediately following them.

ONCE AGAIN, DANIELLE and Steve thought long and hard about how to handle the presentation. They had already played the "clever" card, now they had to put some meat on the bones. The timeline was tight so they pulled some long nights and researched the heck out of similar organizations in Europe and how they had handled attracting corporate sponsorships. Building on this information, they put together a unique approach to monetizing the organization's assets.

Then Steve stumbled on an extensive article, based on a brand-new report, by a leading expert in corporate sponsorship for heritage sites in Great Britain and Ireland. In it were some fascinating statistics and research, along with some groundbreaking observations and recommendations. They decided to use this information to weaken what they considered their competition's credibility advantage. On the day of the presentation, they walked into the room and plugged their laptop into the projector (earlier, they had already made sure that it was compatible and ready to go). Their first few slides were of several heritage sites featuring the logos of the organizations that managed them; each slide featured statistics relevant to the goals and objectives of the organization with which they were hoping to work. Surprisingly, when Danielle faced the audience, she recognized someone; he was seated at the back of the room, not at the boardroom table so she surmised that he was acting as an observer. Their eyes briefly made contact and he gave her an encouraging smile.

As she had in the previous presentation, Danielle went over the key information in a few slides, this time with some added details. It was then that she delivered what she and Steve hoped would once again help them stand out from their competition; she said, "The strategies being used right now to attract corporate sponsorship for organizations just like yours in Europe are light years ahead of what is happening here in the United States. Any company expecting, or even trying, to meet the expectations outlined in your RFP is going to have to have a clear understanding of . . ." What she then outlined came directly from the report Steve had discovered and contained powerful observations and unique strategies that had proven to be highly successful. The statement was a bit of a stretch, but there was no doubt that what they had learned from the European report and their subsequent research would be immensely useful should they be awarded the contract. When she finished, several members of the committee immediately burst into applause. She knew she had done the best job she could under the circumstances.

The following day she received a call from the person she had recognized; he told her that their presentation had been very warmly received. He also said that the other company did little to alter their presentation and simply reemphasized their size and experience. Her contact went on to tell her that the first question the committee asked her competition was, what did they know about the strategies that Danielle said would be "necessary" for any company hoping to deliver on the contract to adopt? Apparently, the other team had never heard of the European report, and they were completely caught off guard. Danielle's "spy" reported that once the company left the room, the committee made a very quick decision to award the contract to Danielle and Steve.

THE ACT OF selling, or making a sale, is not always about one visit, one person, one sale; when the stakes are high you will need to meet multiple times with prospects and find a way to combat the strengths of the competition and use their weaknesses against them. In this case, Danielle knew the larger, more established company had little respect for her company and therefore underestimated their resourcefulness. They had relied almost exclusively on their past credibility and failed to focus on the needs of the client. Danielle and Steve out-researched them and simply came armed with a better strategy—a strategy based on current industry knowledge that convinced the organization they were better prepared and qualified to deliver on the contract, despite their size and the limited time they had been in business.

ˇ   *The act of selling, or making a sale, is not always about*
ˇ   *one visit, one person, one sale; when the stakes are high*
ˇ   *you will need to meet multiple times with prospects and*
ˇ   *find a way to combat the strengths of the competition*
ˇ   *and use their weaknesses against them.*

How Not to Sell

- Always arrive just in time; if you're too early it looks like you are needy.
- Use PowerPoints with at least twenty bullets per slide written in 10-point font—that way you can pack more information into your presentation. People don't need to be able to read your slides. You can read them out loud—most prospects are illiterate anyway.
- Funky fonts are fun and will keep your audience on their toes as they try to make out the words.
- People enjoy quirky clip art and humorous photographs in formal presentations: it keeps them alert.
- If ten slides are good, fifty are better.
- Excel spreadsheets look impressive in a PowerPoint presentation. A blurry screengrab works well—after all, you don't want anyone to actually read it.
- Focus on you and your company and ignore your potential buyer's needs.

TWENTY-SEVEN

How Dare They Object!

Handling objections is at the heart of successful selling. So long as there is an objection lingering in the prospect's mind, the salesperson is unlikely to close the deal. Few salespeople grasp the simple fact that if there are zero objections remaining then they have the sale—assuming they ask for it, of course.

Problems arise when a salesperson thinks they have addressed all of the prospect's objections, when in reality, there are several that have been left unrecognized and unanswered.

The single biggest issue with salespeople is that they are either afraid of hearing objections or take them as an insult. What they should be doing is welcoming, even encouraging, them.

> ∨ *The single biggest issue with salespeople is that they*
> ∨ *are either afraid of hearing objections or take them as*
> ∨ *an insult. What they should be doing is welcoming, even*
> ∨ *encouraging, them.*

Here's a wonderful tale about a realtor named Gary who became indignant whenever someone dared to criticize what he was selling. First, however, we'll need some background on his prospects, Nicole and Joshua. Nicole is a successful chartered accountant and Joshua owns a tech company. In this story, Nicole talks about the time they were house hunting and decided to look at a house while out for a weekend drive.

JOSH AND I spotted the open house sign while driving around looking at areas where we thought we'd like to live. This particular house stood out immediately—it was new and exactly what we were looking for, at least based on its curb appeal. As we entered the foyer, we noticed a large tiled mural of an eagle on the floor; the first thing we both thought was that it looked a little like the presidential seal. The realtor was in the kitchen talking to another potential buyer, so we just wandered through the house, eventually ending up in the kitchen, which was enormous but poorly laid out. Counters ran the length of one wall—they seemed to go on for twenty feet or more, and I could imagine walking from end to end a dozen times while cooking a meal.

By this time the other person had left, and the realtor introduced himself to us as Gary Sheldrake and shook our hands. Before we exchanged any other pleasantries he asked what we thought of the eagle. "Isn't it amazing?" he said.

Without thinking I replied, "Oh God, no, if we bought this house that would have to go, it's hideous." Josh squeezed my hand tightly and I realized I probably could have been more diplomatic about how I felt.

Gary's demeanor changed instantly. His face went red and he almost shouted, "But, but, that's a work of art; it was designed by a well-known local artist. You can't destroy a work of art."

I hate being told what I can and can't do so despite Josh's grip getting tighter I replied, "Watch me. If we were to buy this house, I'd expect the developer to get rid of it before we moved in."

Gary was now apoplectic; it was like I was insulting him personally, and I seriously thought he was going to burst a blood vessel. At that point I knew we were never going to buy this house even though it did have potential. Sensing this, Josh decided to push a few of Gary's buttons and asked, "What's with the kitchen? Whoever designed it has never cooked a meal in their life; it's an ergonomic disaster."

To his credit, Gary did try to hide his frustration a little and said, through gritted teeth, that most people who came through the house loved it, but if it wasn't to our taste he could see whether the developer would be prepared to redesign it. As a parting shot, he said he had other houses that might better suit our needs.

We were fed up with Gary's attitude, though, and while we felt a little guilty about teasing him we had no intention of giving him our business. Looking back, that house might have worked for us—it was the right size and the kitchen was so large it would have been relatively easy for the developer to add an island and rearrange some of the cabinets. Even the damn eagle wouldn't have been a deal breaker—we could have covered it with a rug. But that ridiculous realtor getting all bent out of shape and offended just because our taste in art was different from his simply put us off completely.

GARY COULD HAVE handled things a lot differently: the fact that Nicole and Joshua were commenting on the mural and the kitchen meant that they were at least considering the house as an option. Gary should have said something like, "Yes, the eagle's not to everyone's taste. If it's a deal breaker I'm sure the developer would consider removing it and matching the tile with the rest of the foyer." After all, it was not as if Gary was going to have to live there—all he had to do was sell the house. The same goes for the kitchen; as the heart of the home, if Nicole was considering how it might work on a day-to-day basis, she was clearly interested. Getting the developer to do some relatively minor alterations to the space to meet a buyer's needs is not a big deal when a home is worth several million dollars. Why Gary took the objections as an attack on his "product" is anyone's guess. Perhaps he was having difficulty selling the house. Maybe he really liked the house the way it was and wished he could buy it himself. Perhaps he simply didn't have answers to their objections or he was jealous that they were successful and wealthy, or he thought they weren't serious buyers. Maybe he was just a jerk. The bottom line is that he lost a potential sale because he never learned how to handle objections correctly. More than that, he lost the opportunity of showing Nicole and Joshua other homes in the area.

How Not to Sell

- If someone raises an objection, ignore it—they'll forget about it before you get to ask for the order.
- Rude prospects need to be put in their place; you are right to take offense if they are being negative about what you sell, and it's okay to show anger toward them.
- Protect the integrity of what you sell at all costs—tell buyers they don't know what they are talking about if they dare to criticize you, your products, or your company.

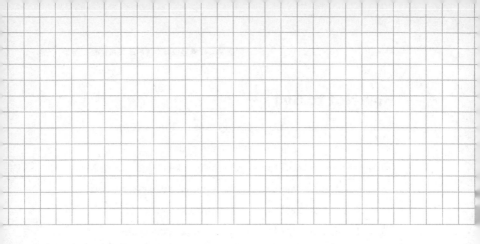

TWENTY-EIGHT

People Are Just Being Awkward When They Raise Objections

Trust, or rather a lack of it, is often a key reason why someone might raise an objection. The prospect may have doubts about you or your company's ability to deliver. This can be for myriad reasons—they might have heard something detrimental about your company, or perhaps they had a negative experience with a colleague. Your credibility, and that of your company and what it sells, are major factors when you're dealing with objections.

Before you can start to manage objections in the field, you need to understand what people are thinking when they raise an objection and also learn to identify the four primary types of objections (real, accidental, false, and hidden).

∨ *Before you can start to manage objections in the field,*
∨ *you need to understand what people are thinking when*
∨ *they raise an objection and also learn to identify the*
∨ *four primary types of objections (real, accidental, false,*
∨ *and hidden).*

There is always the chance that a prospect is just being awkward and raising objections just for the sake of it, but in reality, there is almost always a reason. Here, too, some of the reasons can relate to whether the person is Analytical, Driven, Expressive, or Amiable.

Many people simply need more information before they make a decision. In this case the questions they raise and the statements they make may not, in the truest sense, be objections; they may in effect reflect a genuine need for further information (especially if they are an Analytical or an Amiable buyer).

Some raise objections because they are seeking validation; they are testing themselves as much as the salesperson, and they actually want to be convinced that they are about to make the right decision. In other words, they are looking for reassurances. Remarks such as, "It's not going to be powerful enough to meet my needs" come across as objections but might really be a cry for assurance that the product will indeed meet their needs.

People on the Analytical end of the spectrum need to demonstrate their expertise and test that of the salesperson with statements like, "I hear that your competitor has a more effective solution," for instance. They actively seek the pros and cons of each alternative and hope to obtain them by raising objections.

In some cases, objections are raised on behalf of people who couldn't be present. This can happen when one spouse is responsible for buying something that the whole household will use and they need to fully brief the absent partner. Some people are naturally suspicious of all companies and salespeople and will raise objections by way of criticism. This can present itself in an objection such as, "I heard your company regularly fails to meet delivery dates."

Certain people have a need to negotiate or barter in order to feel like they are getting a good deal. Their objections come in the form of negative comments, such as, "I'm not sure I like the color," or "I've seen this down the road for less money."

Then we have the know-it-alls: these people want to test your knowledge because they have to prove that they know more than you do. Their objections will often be technical: "You claim this car will get 30 mpg in the city and 38 on the highway, but *Motor Trend* magazine says otherwise." They just want to make you work hard for the sale—it's like a game to them. They're often salespeople themselves. Don't expect professional courtesy when selling to fellow salespeople: they can be the most judgmental prospects of all.

> ∨ *Don't expect professional courtesy when selling to*
> ∨ *fellow salespeople: they can be the most judgmental*
> ∨ *prospects of all.*

So, there are lots of reasons people object, but one thing you need to be able to do before you manage their objection is figure out what type of objection you are dealing with.

Real Objections

These are the easiest objections to deal with as you'll have heard them in the past so you should know how to answer them. If a new real objection is raised and you don't have a way to overcome it, you can tell the prospect or buyer that you will get back to them with an answer. Of course, some real objections can't be overcome, such as when someone tells you they can get the same product and service at your competitors for less money. If you can't point to some added value that sets you apart, then it's an objection you won't be able to satisfactorily speak to. You should, however, take a long look at your pricing or value proposition and make changes, so that in the future this objection either cannot be raised or you'll have a compelling counterargument.

There is another reason why you may not be able to answer a real objection and that's because what you are selling is not suitable for your buyer. For instance, if you are trying to sell a nine-foot long couch to someone living in a seven-hundred-square-foot condo, you're putting yourself into a no-win situation. You need to ask yourself: Did I qualify my prospect sufficiently?

Examples of real objections include:

- I think it might be a little big for my office/living room/ garage, etc.
- It's really ugly.
- I was expecting more bells and whistles for my money.
- This seems expensive for what it is.
- What if it goes wrong?
- I already have a supplier/financial advisor, etc.
- I read that this model is unreliable.

Accidental Objections

Too often, sales are lost because the salesperson and the prospect are talking at cross-purposes. Somewhere during the sales pitch, the prospect has misunderstood something. In this case the worst thing you can do is tell them they are wrong (remember the earlier story about The Owl and the Beaver Bookshop). If you realize your prospect is operating on a misapprehension, don't tell them they are wrong; simply stop and give a recap, and when you get to the part where a prospect misunderstood what you said, slow down and ensure that this time they hear you clearly.

Examples of accidental objections include:

- There's no way I'm signing a three-year contract.
- I'm not interested unless there's a warranty; I know I can get one from your rival.
- I don't want to repackage and send it away myself if it breaks down.
- You sell to my competition; sorry, but that's a deal breaker.
- No deal; I'm not paying up front.

False Objections

It's easy to think that any objection is false; after all, your product is perfect, right?

The key to handling false objections is to recognize them for what they are: a prospect telling you that they are not yet ready to fully engage with you, or that you are pushing them too hard. When was the last time you went into a used car dealership or a large chain fashion retailer and had one or more salespeople almost launch themselves at you like piranhas in a feeding frenzy? What did you do? You probably told them you were just looking—it's the stock reply that we all say, even if we've entered a store with the specific goal of making a purchase.

Examples of false objections include:

- I'm just looking.
- I can't afford it.
- It's too expensive.
- I'm not ready to buy.

Hidden Objections

Salespeople that suspect an objection is really hiding another more serious concern need to probe and probe again until they discover the real issue. Remember, as long as there is an unspoken objection the sale will almost never occur. We'll talk about handling objections in more detail in the next chapter.

Here are some signs that indicate you might be dealing with a hidden objection.

- When you address an objection and you discover that it was blatantly false, such as the ones listed above under "false objections." If it's false, it's hiding a real objection.
- When the sale is not going anywhere, and you have no idea why. Lack of progress is an obvious sign there is a hidden objection.
- When the prospect keeps coming up with frivolous objections. In this case, they are avoiding bringing up a more serious matter, such as they don't like you or your attitude.
- When the prospect looks uncomfortable, they are usually hiding an objection. This can happen when they have something critical to say about what you are selling

and they don't want to hurt your feelings or get into an argument.

Examples of hidden objections:

• Send me your literature.
• Let me think about it.
• Can I trust you or your company?
• I have to talk to my boss, manager, etc.
• I'll get back to you.

If you are having difficulty identifying the type of objection, consider where your prospect's objection is coming from—is it a genuine concern? Or does it suggest any of the following?

• Difficulty, or even fear, of making commitments (particularly in Amiable personalities).
• Anger at previous treatment—possibly by someone else in your industry.
• Deliberately awkward behavior—this often reflects a desire to make a salesperson's life difficult.
• A desire to show superiority; some individuals have a need to assert their knowledge (Driver and Analytical personalities especially).
• Bartering, which suggests the need for a good or better deal.
• An irresistible desire for more information (often found in Analytical personalities).
• A general lack of confidence in your company's ability to deliver.

- A need to know you better before doing business with you (especially common in Expressive and Amiable personalities).

Rarely does a sale happen quickly unless the buyer has done all their homework and they've already made the purchasing decision before you even meet them. In this case, you are not a salesperson, you are an order taker.

Selling is a process, a negotiation; customers will have questions and concerns, and they will raise issues, which if not resolved, will prevent you from making the sale. Successfully overcoming objections—be they real, accidental, false, or hidden—is a skill every salesperson needs to learn if they are going to have a decent closing rate. In Chapter Twenty-Nine, we'll go into more detail about how to handle those pesky things that are standing between you and your commission.

> ∨   *Selling is a process, a negotiation; customers will have*
> ∨   *questions and concerns, and they will raise issues,*
> ∨   *which if not resolved, will prevent you from making the*
> ∨   *sale. Successfully overcoming objections—be they real,*
> ∨   *accidental, false, or hidden—is a skill every salesperson*
> ∨   *needs to learn if they are going to have a decent*
> ∨   *closing rate.*

How Not to Sell

- Treat all objections identically. They are all the same—
  a pain in the backside.
- There's no such thing as a genuine objection.
- Treat objections as a customer's way of stalling. Push
  through them with your sales pitch—there's nothing to be
  gained from trying to understand the buyer's concerns.
- People are all the same. There's no mileage in trying to
  take their personality type into consideration; use the
  same answers and reasoning on everyone.

TWENTY-NINE

The Best Way to Handle Objections Is to Ignore Them

A great salesperson learns to love objections, and the best way to love them is to find a way not to feel scared or insulted. How do you do that? The best way is to consider every objection that could possibly be raised and prepare an answer in advance. Take some time to think about every objection you've ever heard—whether real, accidental, false, or hidden—and make a list of how you may have successfully addressed them in the past. If you are a member of a sales team, this is a powerful and valuable group activity.

Once you have your list, pull out the ones you dread, those that you have difficulty answering, and figure out a way to handle them;

ask your colleagues, your manager, or even some of your best customers for assistance. Once you have a comprehensive list, you can relax in the knowledge that you can handle those objections—in fact you'll embrace them and of course resolve them effectively.

What follows is a quick course in how to handle objections. You won't be surprised to hear that ignoring them is not going to win you many sales. The first thing you need to do is practice listening—active listening. To overcome an objection, you need to understand both the facts and the motivation behind what is being said. You need to listen carefully so that you can discover what the real objection is, rather than what is being said on the surface.

> ∨   *To overcome an objection, you need to understand*
> ∨   *both the facts and the motivation behind what is being*
> ∨   *said. You need to listen carefully so that you can*
> ∨   *discover what the real objection is, rather than what*
> ∨   *is being said on the surface.*

Once you have achieved this, you need to show the prospect, or customer, that you understand their concern and that you want to find a way to overcome the issue. In most cases, if you did the exercise suggested at the beginning of this chapter, you will have an answer ready at hand. If not, you will need to ask the person to further clarify their concerns. Quite often this exercise results in them coming up with their own solution or possibly realizing that their reservation is not a deal-breaking issue.

When dealing with objections, active listening works like magic; nodding your head, and making affirmative sounds such as, "hmm, I see, yes," encourages the prospect to feel safe and open up about their concerns and ultimately reveal hidden objections. Take note of any emotion in their voice and then take action; for in-stance, you might say something like, "You seem concerned about ..." or, "It appears that ... is worrying you."

- ∨ *When dealing with objections, active listening works*
- ∨ *like magic; nodding your head, and making affirmative*
- ∨ *sounds such as, "hmm, I see, yes," encourages the*
- ∨ *prospect to feel safe and open up about their concerns*
- ∨ *and ultimately reveal hidden objections.*

Paraphrase what the person is saying and ask clarification ques-tions; this demonstrates that not only are you listening, but you care and are invested in finding a solution. Maintain eye contact; remember, trust is important when you are offering solutions, just as it is to closing sales and building solid relationships.

The techniques outlined above will encourage people to open up to you and reveal what's on their mind. But sometimes active listening is not enough. This is where highly successful salespeople kick it up a notch and start actively looking for objections. If this seems contrary to logic, remember what we said earlier about the objection being the only thing preventing a sale; if every objection has been answered, the sale is yours. So, why wouldn't you mine for them? Ask questions such as: Am I right in sensing that you have some concerns? Have you purchased this type of product/service before? Have you ever used/tried a product/service like this in the past? Do you see any downsides to this product/service? Consider what other questions might assist you in gathering information that would help you make a sale. The basic issue behind almost all objections is that the customer believes the financial cost out-weighs the value offered by what you are trying to sell them.

The solution to this is fourfold: First, find out what the customer means by value. Second, show the features, advantages, and benefits of your product and place a value on them. Third, encourage the customer to examine the total cost of ownership, not simply the purchase cost, and fourth, take the buyer through the features and link benefits to each.

Managing Objections—A Quick Review

- Listen
- Acknowledge
- Assess
- Empathize
- Understand
- Respond
- Confirm
- Repeat (if necessary)

How Not to Sell

- Don't prepare for objections ahead of time—it's fun to be put on the spot.
- Make sure you point out the stupidity of the customer's objections.
- Objections are always about price not value, so resort to discounting if the going gets tough.
- The best way to deal with an objection is to change the subject. The prospect will forget about it once you hit them with all the good things about your product, or you tell them a joke.

- An outstanding objection won't stop you from getting an order; just bully your prospect into buying.
- If a prospect mentions your competition, slam the other company quickly and mercilessly.

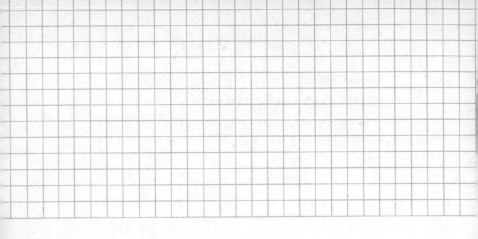

THIRTY

Closing Is Just a Matter of Going in for the Kill

Closing is often thought to be the toughest and scariest part of selling. The truth is, it doesn't need to be. If you've followed the advice in every chapter, then you should be able to position yourself in such a way as to make the sale a natural conclusion to your interaction with your prospect or customer. Closing is the natural climax to the interaction—the buyer knows it and the salesperson knows it, so why should it be the elephant in the room?

In fact, closing should take place right from the beginning of the interaction between a salesperson and the buyer. ABC (Always Be Closing) is a common mantra in books on selling and deserves repeating—if it isn't broke, don't fix it.

> ∨   *In fact, closing should take place right from the*
> ∨   *beginning of the interaction between a salesperson*
> ∨   *and the buyer. ABC (Always Be Closing) is a common*
> ∨   *mantra in books on selling and deserves repeating—*
> ∨   *if it isn't broke, don't fix it.*

There's a lot that can go wrong in the sales process, but it is particularly galling when you fall at the final hurdle and walk away with nothing to show for all your effort; when you've done everything by the book and the buyer is interested but you can't close the deal. Sometimes it's because you are scared of being rejected, and often it's because there's a hidden objection you haven't discovered. Sometimes it's because you haven't spotted the buying signals. And then there's the biggest reason of all: you can't bring yourself to ask for the order.

Let me tell you a story from my own past. I used to work for an economic development organization. My boss (later my business partner and lifelong friend) was a wonderful man named Ken; he was a genius, at least when it came to other people's businesses. He had a knack of helping others become highly successful—he had more great business ideas while shaving every morning than most of us have in our entire lifetime. He was directly responsible for helping over 2,500 start-ups become successful through a federally funded entrepreneurial program and he was my mentor for over twenty years. But while he was phenomenal at helping other people become successful, he struggled to get his own business ideas to hit the big time.

One of the reasons was that he was almost too kind and generous. He and I developed a business training program aimed at new entrepreneurs. It consisted of a comprehensive manual, which included a wide range of information on everything from writing a business plan to sales and marketing to human resources to goal setting to accounting and law. Dozens of PowerPoint presentations accompanied the manual; and a manned helpline topped off a highly desirable product aimed at government-funded, rural economic development offices delivering business programs and private training schools.

Revenues from the sale of the program were not living up to expectations, so Ken and I decided to go on a sales trip together visiting a dozen towns during a week on the road. It didn't take me long before I knew exactly why our financial situation was precarious. Ken was presenting our product to a rural economic development office; it was the first time I'd seen him make a sales pitch, and he was impressive. His enthusiasm and product knowledge were faultless; his experience and understanding of the subject matter contained in the manual were exemplary. He even spouted off facts and statistics about every town we visited, giving unsolicited but valuable economic development advice to everyone we met. I was witnessing the power of a master sales presenter. I was in awe. Right up until I saw our prospect desperately trying to commit to purchasing the program, only to see Ken say, "Well, as you know, this program is usually $1,599 a year, but for you I'm sure we could shave 30 percent off that figure." I was stunned; sure, we got the order, but a chunk of our profit went out the window. I was mentally adding up the cost of hotel rooms, gas, and food for the trip and could see that if this continued, the more Ken sold, the more money we'd lose.

At dinner that night, we discussed the situation and he promised he would do better the following day. Unfortunately, Ken choked every time the order was within reach; he couldn't close the deal when it was right in front of him, so I started kicking him hard under the table whenever I felt that he should shut up. Then I would take over and say, quite simply, "Mr. Smith, when would you like to start delivering the program in your community?" Done deal—that was all it took. Once I spotted the moment the prospect had sufficient information and was giving us buying signals, I closed Ken and his presentation down and moved on to the paperwork.

In the sales world, closing has a bad rap. It's like it's evil or sleazy—people will hate you for closing the sale and getting the order. Ken wanted to be liked, he wanted to be the good guy, he genuinely wanted to help people. Unfortunately, you can only help people if you remain in business and to do that you have to make profitable sales—lots of them.

In the story above, Ken either missed the buying signals altogether or was so invested in his sales pitch that he couldn't stop. Here's one more story, a positive one this time, about closing. Again, it's from my own history and again took place during the period I worked for Ken.

I was selling corporate sponsorships to support Ken's economic development association and had "sold" Derek, a local bank manager, on sponsoring the organization; the only hitch was that he had to sell *his* boss, the regional vice president.

He suggested that I make the pitch myself during the intermission at a charity dinner concert the VP was attending. True to his word, Derek sought me out and I was told I had two minutes to convince the VP that this was the right thing for them to support. Derek had built me up to his boss; he had told him that I was an excellent salesperson and that he should see me in action. As flattering as this was, it put me firmly in the VP's crosshairs—I was on trial.

I was well prepared and knew my presentation had to be concise and on point. I started outlining the benefits the bank would get from the alliance and how it would fit their marketing strategy and the ways in which we would ensure they got their money's worth. All the time I was making the presentation, I was studying the man, particularly his eyes. One minute in, I stopped and said, "I don't need to continue; you just decided to buy." His mouth dropped open, he looked at his colleague, and said, "Unbelievable. He's right; just this second I thought, 'Yep we'll do this.'"

He turned to me and asked me how I could possibly know. I told him that his shoulders relaxed, his confrontational (possibly faked) attitude changed, his eyes softened, and there was the merest twinkle of a smile in them.

Now, many of my students over the years have said that I must have second sight or something, but that doesn't have anything to do with it; anyone can "see" when the person in front of them has been "sold"—you just have to look for the signals. If you take the time to practice identifying buying signs, you will be able to create that same result and surprise your buyers with your "psychic" ability.

Buying signals can be as obvious as someone getting their checkbook out of their briefcase, or as subtle as the VP's demeanor in the story above. Learning how to recognize these signals is an important skill if you expect to be successful as a sales professional.

In Chapter Twenty-Six, Samantha told us her story about selling video games and how her sales trainer told her she had missed her customer's buying signals, which resulted in a reduced order.

The graphic below illustrates the journey a sale makes in the mind of a buyer. The left and right hemispheres of the brain process information in different ways. Individually, we might lean more toward left- or right-brain thinking, but for the most part the two sides work together to help us function and make decisions. Left-brain thinking is verbal and analytical. Right-brain thinking is nonverbal and intuitive, using pictures rather than words.

- The right brain deals with creativity, imagination, holistic thinking, intuition, the arts, rhythms, nonverbal feelings, and visualization, to name a few.
- The left brain deals with logic, analysis, sequencing, math, language, and facts—it works in a linear fashion.

When listening to your sales pitch or presentation, buyers usually begin in right-brain mode as shown on the graph. It is only later that their left brain kicks in.

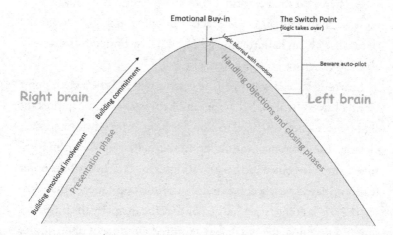

Assuming you are not on a cold call and your prospect is at least somewhat receptive to your message and interested in what you are selling, they are likely to be visualizing the features, advantages, and benefits of your product or service and how it might suit their needs. They might be imagining how their customers will respond and whether it could be a good seller—or how their employees might respond to using the equipment or machinery you are proposing. At this point you have an opportunity to encourage your prospect to build an emotional attachment to whatever it is you are selling. As you provide more information and talk about features, advantages, and benefits, the buyer's commitment should be growing—assuming you are doing a good job. They are buying into your message and the idea of placing an order. Interestingly, at this point—because they are using their right brain—they are less likely to be thinking about price or other negative factors. Eventually, however, they reach the switch point—the moment where the left brain kicks in and logic enters the picture and begins to influence their thinking.

It is here that their emotional buy-in can come into conflict with logic, analysis, and other hard facts. Thoughts such as, "Do I really need this?" "Can I afford this right now?" "I wonder if this is available less expensively somewhere else."

Learning to read when you are getting close to the switch point from a buyer's words, behavior, and expressions is an important skill. This is when you need to stop pitching or presenting and start closing. The moments leading up to the switch point are an ideal time to look for objections, use trial closes, or even ask for the order if appropriate. Every second after that prime point means that closing the sale is going to get harder, or that the quantity the buyer has in mind is falling. Every sale has a limited window of opportunity as the prospect's brain becomes embroiled in doubts and reasons why the purchase might not be such a good idea. Control the switch point and you control the sale.

> ∨ Learning to read when you are getting close to the
> ∨ switch point from a buyer's words, behavior, and
> ∨ expressions is an important skill. This is when you
> ∨ need to stop pitching or presenting and start closing.
> ∨ The moments leading up to the switch point are an
> ∨ ideal time to look for objections, use trial closes, or
> ∨ even ask for the order if appropriate.

Think of all the times you have thought about buying something—maybe a new car, or a luxury vacation, or an original piece of art. How many times were you ready to place the order, make the commitment, but decided to sleep on it and then ultimately backed off? It is human nature to get enthusiastic about something that sounds wonderful; occasionally we'll make an impulse purchase, but more often than not—especially with higher-priced items—given time, we will convince ourselves not to make the purchase.

> ∨ It is human nature to get enthusiastic about something
> ∨ that sounds wonderful; occasionally we'll make an
> ∨ impulse purchase, but more often than not—especially
> ∨ with higher-priced items—given time, we will convince
> ∨ ourselves not to make the purchase.

Closing is a journey. Before you decide to ask for the order, you can use trial closes as a stress-free way of testing the waters. Since prospects' buying signals are not always obvious, you have to be prepared to give them a little nudge now and again. Trial closes are a great way to get an idea of how your sales presentation or pitch is being received. They're often forgotten—even by experienced salespeople—but their power cannot be underestimated.

A trial close focuses on one or more questions that help you gauge how serious your prospect is about buying whatever you're selling. Their answers may be in the form of objections, which, as we learned earlier, is a good thing. Remember, we have to answer all of those lovely objections before we can get a sale.

There's no set time to carry out a trial close and you really can't go wrong, but the key is not to make your questions sound too pushy. Trial closes are a low-risk, high-reward strategy because you'll get an opinion from your prospect (hopefully positive). On the other hand, a full close asks the person for an immediate buying decision. Remember when you use a trial close you should be looking for changes in the behavior, demeanor, and attitude of the buyer. Think back to the story about the vice president of the bank in the previous chapter.

Trial close questions can be just about anything. Here are a few examples:

- Does this fit your needs?
- Is there anything else you'd like to know about?
- What is most important to you about our product?
- How close are we to meeting your needs?
- Does the price seem reasonable?
- Is the price within your budget?
- When would you need delivery?
- Do you prefer the silver or white iPhone?
- What would you see as the next step?

- Would you need to get your manager to sign off on this type of purchase?

Think of trial closes as soft closes. If you ask your prospect when they might want the delivery and they answer, "Could you get it here by the twentieth?" that is a clear buying signal that can immediately lead to a close.

Watch for buying signals when using trial closes. These include:

- A change of attitude—the buyer becomes friendlier and more open.
- The buyer leans forward, becomes more engaged, and asks questions relating to things like shipping options and discounts for bulk purchases.
- The buyer becomes more animated vocally—they show excitement, their voice goes up an octave, conveying enthusiasm, or possibly down a bit, suggesting that they are serious.
- The prospect's eyes brighten, showing that they are keen, or their gaze becomes more relaxed indicating they have made a decision.

If you use trial closes effectively, then your road to getting the order is going to be smoother and you will likely be able to use the easiest close in the book, the assumption close. In the example above where the salesperson asked the prospect when they might want delivery and they replied with a question about a specific date, the salesperson could have used the assumption close and said, "Yes, I can make that happen. I'll write the order up right now and email it to the warehouse immediately." Job done.

The key to closing is to deal with objections before the switch point, while the prospect or buyer is still in right-brain mode and emotional buy-in is still strong. If you can do this, you will find they approach objections from a positive rather than a negative perspective. It's your choice: let the buyer free-flow on autopilot or control the narrative.

How Not to Sell

- The best way to close is to back the prospect into a corner so they can't say no.
- Don't look for the buying signals; buyers are inscrutable. It's a fallacy that you can tell if someone is ready to buy what you're selling.
- Left brain, right brain—it's all psychobabble.
- If you think you spot a buying signal, either ignore it and keep hammering home the benefits or start discounting like crazy to ensure you get the sale.
- Never use trial closes—they are just a trick. Allow the buyer tons of time to make their decision.

THIRTY-ONE

Buyers Will Tell Me When They're Ready to Buy— No Need to Close

Whether you ask for the order as a result of a series of trial closes, which lead you to believe that your prospect is ready to make a positive decision, or you simply know they are ready, you still have to choose how you are going to close the sale. There are many types of closes and you'll have to decide which one works for you based on your personality, the type of product or service you are selling, or the type of prospect, buyer, or business you are selling to. The two most common closes in the list below are the assumption close and simply just asking for the order.

- **Assumption Close**—An assumption close is exactly what it sounds like: the salesperson assumes he/she has the order and starts writing it up, or discussing delivery details, or colors, or whatever. The key to using this close is to conduct enough trial closes to be confident that the buyer has made their decision, even if they haven't said so in so many words.

- **Specific Terms Close**—This is an offshoot of the assumption close where the salesperson says something like, "Okay, we can deliver the training program you require any day the week after next, at $75 a head with the workbooks costing $20 each. Shall I reserve that date for you?" At this point the buyer may start saying something like, "The week after next is too soon . . ." By that time, the sale is in the bag and the salesperson is just handling the details.

- **The Return Question Close**—If a buyer inquires about product options and asks, "Does this come in silver?" the salesperson's reply should be, "Would you like to place an order for it in that color?"

- **Free Trial Close**—The salesperson might say something like, "I'll tell you what, why don't you take it on trial for a week and we can write up the order later?" At that point they treat it exactly as they would a sale. The buyer can cancel later, but if they've agreed to the trial, that's unlikely, unless the product/service proves unsatisfactory.

- **Deadline Close**—This is a common close in retail that can rely on almost continuous time-limited sales to encourage customers to commit to a purchase immediately. Salespeople will say, "This offer only applies while stock lasts, so would you like to order now to secure this price?"

- **Dangle Close**—In this case the salesperson might say, "I'm not sure I can get it in that color," or "I may not be able to make that date," or "I don't think we have that many available, but I can check, and if we do, shall I put it on hold for you?"

- **This or That Close**—This is a simple close, where the salesperson proactively suggests options, asking, "Would you prefer the red or the blue? The twenty-four or thirty-six pack?"

- **Recommendation Close**—This works well when the salesperson has gained the buyer's complete trust. They simply say something such as, "I would suggest you order x number of y and z. I guarantee that will best meet your needs." It works particularly well when selling to Amiable personalities but can often work with Drivers. This close is all about trust: trust in the sales professional and trust in the product/service.

- **Pros and Cons Close**—This close often works well with Analytical personalities. The salesperson works with the prospect to draw up a list of the pros and cons of their product against the other options open to the prospect. Hopefully, strong logic will prevail and guide the person to the sale. The salesperson can then say, "Well, that certainly shows this is your best option; you just need to let me know how many you require (or when you want them delivered)."

- **Ask for the Order**—This is probably the most honest and straightforward close of all. If a sales professional has done their job well—that is, identified a need and want; confirmed the buyer has the authority to make the purchase and that they can afford the asking price; presented all of the product's features, advantages, and benefits; and finally managed to answer every objection— then the only thing left to do is say, "Great, can I write the order up for you?"

In Chapter Four, we discussed the various social, or behavioral styles—when closing it is a good idea to take this into consideration. Closing by social style can have a significant impact on your closing rate.

Closing an Analytical

- Start at the end and provide a process.
- Use Pros and Cons or Deadline closes.

Closing a Driver

- Demonstrate how they can make or save money, time, effort, or resources.
- Assumption close (or just give them room to buy).

Closing an Expressive

- Be their friend and assume you have the order.
- Assumption close.

Closing an Amiable

- Build the relationship, build trust.
- Ensure they have a warranty/guarantee and will have your ongoing support.
- Recommendation close.

Here's a story that illustrates the difficulty people, especially those new to sales, find in closing. In this case, a salesman with a Canadian company that sells timesheets and project management software couldn't even close an introduction.

"One of the first ever calls I did, I had a coworker of mine, who had been with the company for a few years, listen in and give me some feedback. I placed the call and a woman picked up, at which point I asked for the person on my contact list. She let me know he no longer worked for the company. Rather than ask her who would be the best person to connect with, I simply thanked her and immediately hung up the phone. Nerves definitely got the better of me whenever someone actually answered. Needless to say, my coworker got a great laugh out of it. I'm not sure if I ever called them again, but three years later I still get a good laugh from it. Everyone has to start somewhere."

How Not to Sell

- Never ask for the order—if the prospect wants to buy, they will go out of their way to insist you take their order.
- String together a series of questions the prospect can only say yes to, then ask for the order. Works every time.
- Leave closing until the last minute; people are never ready to buy until you are just about to leave.

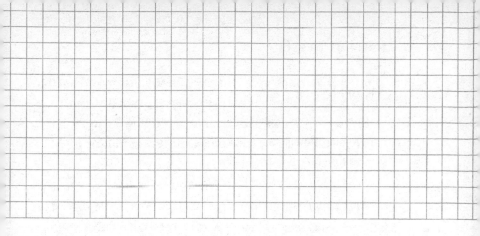

THIRTY-TWO

I Don't Like to Follow Up;
It's Like Stalking

It would be nice to think that every interaction with a prospect results in a sale but in reality there are dozens of things that can delay the close, even if you have done everything correctly throughout the entire sales process and the prospect has every intention of making the purchase. In fact, it might not be that you haven't got the sale—it may simply be that your buyer has yet to provide official confirmation. That is why it is imperative to follow up on every sales call.

Depending on which source you believe, acquiring a new customer can be five to seven times more expensive than selling to an existing customer. The same logic applies to leads and prospects; there is a cost to all the work and effort you put into turning a lead into a prospect and a prospect into a potential customer. Don't waste it; perseverance and tenacity are integral to good salesmanship. Here's a story about perseverance and following up, from Paige, who owns a well-established marketing consulting firm.

IN THE EARLY days of my business, I attended a networking event and unexpectedly discovered that a prospect (a CEO) who I had pitched a month previously was the keynote speaker. Her topic centered on being a woman leader in a traditionally male-dominated business. I had followed up several times via email and voicemail after sending her my proposal but never received a response, so I was a little nervous that my appearance might be construed as an attempt to stalk her, even though I felt that, up to that point, I had just been pleasantly persistent.

You can imagine my shock when she announced at the event, as part of her speech, that she believes it is important to put your money where your mouth is and for women CEOs to support other respected and well-run women's businesses, and that this is why she had hired my firm to handle all of her company's marketing and PR! After her keynote, many people came up and congratulated me; it was a better endorsement than being mentioned in the *New York Times* because she was very well known and had a reputation for having very high standards and being very tough. I got a lot of business from people in the room who thought that if I was able to impress the keynote speaker, I must be very good at what I do. It's amazing to think I almost didn't show up to the event, and also that maybe seeing me there was what prompted her to pull the trigger and hire my firm. Perseverance obviously pays off.

THERE ARE MANY ways you can follow up on a sales call without appearing pushy or becoming a nuisance to your prospect. In fact, follow-ups can and should become part of relationship building. For instance, it's natural to follow up every sales contact with an email thanking them for their time and maybe also recapping what occurred or was agreed to during the meeting.

> ∨ *There are many ways you can follow up on a sales call*
> ∨ *without appearing pushy or becoming a nuisance to*
> ∨ *your prospect. In fact, follow-ups can and should*
> ∨ *become part of relationship building.*

During the sales process, and over the period of time you've known the prospect or customer, you will have had an opportunity to gather information. This information is not only valuable in building the relationship—it is also gold when it comes to following up with customers. For instance, if you've learned that the person enjoys whiskey or is a fan of a particular author, you can use this to keep in touch. Perhaps you see that the author has a new book available, or that there is going to be a Scotch whisky tasting event in their town that weekend; a quick email telling them about it keeps you in touch. If this coincides with the wait for confirmation of an order, then you can slip in a question asking them if there is any news on the purchase.

> ∨ *The more you can follow up with customers on a regular*
> ∨ *basis on non-work-specific topics the more you will be*
> ∨ *on their mind and the easier it will be for you to casually*
> ∨ *ask about work matters too.*

The more you can follow up with customers on a regular basis on non-work-specific topics the more you will be on their mind and the easier it will be for you to casually ask about work matters too.

How Not to Sell

- No need to follow up a sales call—they'll call you if they need something.
- Don't bother sending a thank-you note or a recap of the meeting; they'll just send it straight to their junk file.
- It's just as easy and cost-effective to get new customers as it is to resell or upsell to existing customers.
- If you don't hear back from a potential customer in a few days, move on—you don't want them to think you are stalking them.

THIRTY-THREE

Why Would I Follow Up?
I Got the Order

The value of the follow-up call after getting a sale is often underrated; as is the value of regular contact with past customers. So, you've made the sale and the customer is happy; what do you do now? Well, if you are Hannah, not a lot.

Hannah inherited a busy and highly profitable territory from Harold, an established salesman who had retired. Her company sold industrial cleaning products; it was a B2B environment and highly competitive. First, let's hear the story from Harold's perspective and then we'll see the difference thirty-five years in age and maturity can make.

HAROLD WAS OLD school but in the best possible way; he followed up every call with a mailed thank-you note. Not only that, over the years he had built a database of information on his customers; he knew their birthdays and often their kids' birthdays and kept track of special dates such as graduations and anniversaries. He knew their hobbies and interests and how long they'd been with their companies. Over the years, he had sent cards and small gifts when appropriate, and always took care to ask after their families by name. Later, when the internet arrived, Harold had often sent short emails about all sorts of things relating to matters that he thought his customers might be interested. In short, he had built a strong relationship with the vast majority of them. When he announced his retirement, he'd received twenty-five emails, letters, and cards from his customers; some even turned up at the retirement party his colleagues had planned and had cheered when he received his commemorative watch.

He had spent a few weeks with his young replacement before leaving; he could see that Hannah was keen and knew the company's product catalog almost as well as he did. She was good at sales too; she dressed professionally, had no tattoos (that he could see), and his customers liked her. He felt like he was leaving his customers in good hands.

Hannah was thrilled to have been chosen to take over Harold's territory. It was a prize; he had been working it for decades and had some of the company's biggest customers. That being said, she felt she could do better. Harold had relied heavily on servicing his existing customers but focused far less on bringing on new accounts. In the first three months she had brought on a dozen new accounts, and within six months that had increased to thirty. She worked long hours and by the end of the year she had brought in forty-five new clients. At her year-end evaluation, her sales manager, David, applauded her for all her hard work and congratulated her on bringing in so much new business. Hannah beamed, until David added, "However, your overall territory's revenues have dropped by 12 percent." She felt her heart sink; she felt sick. How could that possibly be? For the next hour they went over her figures. Yes, she had brought in a lot of new clients, but most of them were fairly small. After all, the company was well established and Harold had worked the territory for a very long time. As the post-mortem of her first year dragged on, it got increasingly gory. David told her that during the year the sales revenues of approximately 30 percent of the territory's key customers had dropped significantly, in some cases as much as 60 percent. In addition, several were no longer customers at all. He assured her that the company had expected some attrition due to Harold's popularity, but this level of churn was beyond what was acceptable.

For the next hour or so, David examined her territory from every angle. In the end they both decided that the loss of revenue was directly attributable to reduced sales from some of Harold's best customers. Hannah all of a sudden realized what had happened. In her desire to impress her bosses and to increase the territory's revenues quickly, she had focused on doing just that by bringing in new business. At the same time, however, she had stopped following up regularly with her existing customers. The solid, loyal customers Harold had tried so hard to build a relationship with over the years had started to feel neglected and some began to purchase from the company's competitors. Their loyalty had been more toward Harold than the company and Hannah had not continued the level of care and follow-up established by her predecessor. How could she? She was too busy bringing in new business.

HANNAH IS A good salesperson and today she is a regional manager with another major B2B corporation. Unfortunately, when she was less experienced, her ambition outstripped her common sense; she looked for shiny new business while ignoring the customers who were the foundation of her territory's revenue.

Never undervalue existing customers, and never underestimate the power of following up, not just on a specific sales call but continually throughout the life of a client relationship. Your competitors are always looking for a way to steal your business; don't hand it to them on a plate.

How Not to Sell

- Don't bother to thank them for their order; the prospect will have forgotten you by the time they get their product.
- Never follow up to see if the order arrived in good condition. Don't tempt fate—the prospect might want to send it back.
- Prospects don't want you to keep in touch; it's not as if they are likely to buy from a competitor. Besides, there are all those shiny new prospects out there waiting for your attention.

THIRTY-FOUR

Selling When the Power Has Shifted

Back in the 1950s, salespeople had all the power; today that power has shifted to the customer. Never before have salespeople had to sell to such knowledgeable people. Customers today are not bound to any one supplier or geographic location: they can find products online, they can price match in seconds, and they can read and post product reviews at will.

As discussed in the Introduction, there have been dozens of sales techniques and strategies introduced over the years and many of them have at least some value, but if you sweep aside all the gimmicks and tricks, the basics of selling are quite simple.

In one way or another, the salespeople featured in our "how-not-to" stories failed in one or more of the following areas.

Successful Salespeople
in the Twenty-First Century:

- Are well-informed
- Are trustworthy and display high integrity
- Sell to people who want and need what they are selling
- Sell to people who have the power to buy
- Sell to people who can afford to make the purchase
- Understand their customers' personality types and build effective relationships
- Know the objective of each sales opportunity
- Discover what their customers need
- Partner with the buyer in the decision-making process
- Know in advance all potential objections
- Listen more than they talk
- Use open-ended questions
- Use probing questions
- Search for issues and concerns (objections)
- Dig deeper in order to see the underlying issue (hidden objections)
- Are not pushy and only sell something when it's the correct decision for the buyer
- Effectively use trial close questions
- Know when and how to ask for the order
- Keep in long-term contact with their customers
- Are welcomed back by the customer as a resource

When it gets right down to it, today's successful salesperson is likable, reliable, and oozes integrity. This professional understands people and can style-shift effectively, so customers feel that they are interacting with a kindred spirit; the sales experience is exactly what they are comfortable with and meets their needs in every way. Our twenty-first-century salesperson loves objections, is alert to buying signals, and knows exactly when a prospect is ready and willing for the close. Sales is only complicated if you let it become more about getting the order and less about meeting your customers' needs.

> ∨ *When it gets right down to it, today's successful*
> ∨ *salesperson is likable, reliable, and oozes integrity. This*
> ∨ *professional understands people and can style-shift*
> ∨ *effectively, so customers feel that they are interacting*
> ∨ *with a kindred spirit; the sales experience is exactly*
> ∨ *what they are comfortable with and meets their needs*
> ∨ *in every way.*

Notes

Section 1

1. W. Clement Stone, *The Success System That Never Fails* (1962).

Chapter 5

1. David Merrill and Roger Reid, *Personal Styles & Effective Performance* (CRC Press, 1981).

Chapter 10

1. Krista Williams, "53 Sales Follow Up Statistics," Zoom Info, December 6, 2017, https://blog.zoominfo.com/sales-follow-up-statistics/.

Chapter 11

1. Mike Wicks, *Hi-Touch Selling* (June 1998, New ed. 2017).

Section 2

1. Rob Liano, "Knowledge is power? No. Knowledge on its own is nothing, but the application of useful knowledge, now that is powerful," Twitter, September 4, 2016, https://twitter.com/robliano/status/772464453287804928.

Chapter 18

1. John Naisbitt, *Megatrends: Ten New Directions Transforming Our Lives* (Grand Central Publishing, 1982).

Section 3

1. Mike Wicks, *Handling Objections and Closing Sales* (Encore Workshops, 2015).

Acknowledgments

I am grateful to all the people who contributed stories or anecdotes about poor salesmanship: either their own, or that which they had to suffer. Many of you asked for anonymity and I will respect that wish here, but you know who you are and how valuable your input was in ensuring this book was grounded in reality.

My special thanks to an extraordinary young woman, Megan Shaw McDonald. Your support in researching stories for this book was invaluable. This book is all the better for your research, editing, and writing skills.

To my old friend Wayne Grier, a RE/MAX realtor, for telling me some great stories about his career in sales, especially the one where he was stopped for speeding but still got the sale. And to

Corina Ludwig, of FunctionFox, for sharing tales of what can go wrong when calling prospects. Also, I'd like to thank Dave Warawa, author of *Shut Up! Stop Talking and Start Making Money* for his support.

I'd specifically like to thank the following people who kindly sent me stories: Kent Lewis (Anvil Media Inc.), your timeshare tale was frighteningly on point; Paige Arnof-Fenn (Mavens & Moguls), for a great story about perseverance; Jessica Magoch (JPM Sales Partners LLC.) for her story about coaching a salesperson who lost sight of what she wanted to happen when meeting with a potential customer.

Finally, I'd like to thank my wife, Sheila, who is always there for me when I'm pulling my hair out over a paragraph that I can't seem to get right, or when the light at the end of the tunnel turns out to be an oncoming train.

—Mike Wicks